The Golden Lions

Written by

John A. Messmer, Jr.

www.createspace.com

Scotts Valley, CA 95066
USA

To Ben and Carol,
from John A. M. Jr.
8/18

This novel is the responsibility of the author.

Although this book is based on true testimonials,
records from the National Archives, and historical
events about the Battle of the Bulge, almost all of the
names of the characters are fictional and have no
relationship to anyone living or dead.

For more information or to order additional books,
please contact:

www.createspace.com
100 Enterprise Way
Suite A200
Scott's Valley, CA 95066
USA

Dedicated to the 106th Division, 422nd Regiment, Company F, and my Dad, who fought bravely during World War II

Prologue

No one will ever know exactly what happened during the Battle of the Bulge. Some memories remain strong, while others have faded over time.

This book is a representation of what happened, which is based off of testimonials and other events from the men, who lived the experience, and other historical facts from the National Archives and other sources.

Many gaps exist in the record and only fragments of information were used to create this story. The threads are accurate with the current available information. Most of the events are true and others fiction to give an overall impression of the battle and the aftermath. The dialogue is obviously fiction but the historical dates and statistics are as accurate as possible.

All the names, except for my Dad and a few others, were changed and none of the characters represent the real soldiers, who fought in the battle. The ones, who survived, are the only ones, who know the truth. My objective is to bring a better understanding of what happened to honor the men, who fought for survival.

Chapter One: The First Hour

After I awoke on Sunday, March 24, 2013, I walked toward the kitchen window. To my surprise, I saw a beautiful snowfall. It was the biggest, since 1982. The scene reminded me of a time in 1944, which was told to me by my Dad. Snow covered the landscape and everything seemed, so peaceful.

The scene was visualized within my mind, like I was transported back in time.

No trouble was expected. Only a few skirmishes were reported along the front. Although some soldiers had feelings of desperation, none expected what was about to happen. Everything seemed normal and all the men conducted their normal activities. All were prepared but none were ready for what was about to happen.

The Battle of the Bulge began on the morning of December the 16th, and everyone's life changed, forever.

Explosions from 88's, tanks, and mortars began early in the morning at about 5:30 AM. The calm, before the storm, ended with a 2,000-gun artillery barrage within the position of Company F and the Siegfried Line. The magnificent trees, which towered through the fog toward the dark and overcast sky swayed from the vibrations. The snow, which covered the landscape, was pelted with debris. The serene appearance of the countryside was corrupted.

Pockets of poorer visibility were in the lower regions. The temperature dipped to 13 degrees Fahrenheit. Even with no breeze, the air was frigid. The cold just lingered over their entrenchments.

The explosions shattered the illusions of peace. The flashes from the bombardment lit the darkness and exposed the reality. The noise from the shelling was deafening. With each impact, shrapnel flew everywhere.

No place of safety existed.

There was an eerie salience, before the bombardment, as men observed from their trench into the distance. The snow gave everything a calm appearance. All was peaceful with no signs of the impending assault. The snow gave a false sense of security and reminded many of the men of happier times with their families.

Before the weather clouded, propaganda was dropped from both sides, which consisted of the normal hype and insults.

The noise from the explosions was unbearable for the American soldiers. The tactic was simple from the Germans perspective. The will of the enemy needed to be diminished, before the assault. The constant annoyance of the shelling from the artillery was the first step toward victory.

Shrapnel flew in various directions, as the trees swayed from the vibrations.

Panzer divisions and infantry were ready for the assault. The German tanks would concentrate their efforts with the 110th and 112th infantry, while the 7th army concentrated on the 106th division.

A combination of other forces was ready in other areas to destroy the enemy.

The Americans had only 4 infantry divisions and 1 armored division, before the attack with about 83,000 men. Their forces numbered over 600,000 during the entire German campaign, while the enemy had about 500,000 troops. Most of the Americans were fresh recruits. The Germans used men from the SS and others of various ages, who were able to fight with many of the survivors from other campaigns.

The German troops were well equipped and trained with the proper winter attire. Many had experiences on the Soviet front. Others were new recruits with training. These men had no actual battle experience. All were prepared with the proper offensive weapons.

By some estimates, the American forces were outnumbered 10 to 1 within the early days of the confrontation.

The men of 106th had a 27-mile front to defend within the Ardenne Forest. They were headquartered at St Vith. A river ran close to their position in the rear. They were in an area, which was called the West Wall of the Siegfried Line by the Schnee Eifel. Pillboxes were on the lengthy boundary between the forces toward the west, which were command centers for the various companies.

The pounding of artillery continued as the men waited in the trench. Some concrete bunkers were used, which were near the frontlines for the higher ranking officers. The chain of command monitored the situation, as the shells exploded on the ground and within the trees.

All personnel were needed for the battle. No was one sparred. The opposition was tremendous. The odds were slim for victory but no one actually knew the strength of the opposition in the distance. Nothing was seen of the enemy.

There were a few defectors from the Germans, who told of the attack. The information was sporadic. Nothing could be done. The men just waited in the snow in their winter gear with their grenades, rifles, pistols, B.A.R's, M-1's, Thompson submachine guns, bazookas, flame-throwers, and mortars, etc.

The differences between the opposing forces with the number of soldiers and technology were significant.

The Americans had medium "thin-armored" tanks with less powerful guns than their opponents. The number on the first day of the invasion was over 240 with over 180 tracked vehicles and close to 400 artillery pieces.

Many of the German tanks were heavily armored but not impossible to defeat with the proper tactics and weapons. The German tanks of various models were overwhelming and more powerful than the opposition.

The element of surprise was the Germans main advantage.

Their purpose was to split the American and British forces, capture the main supply line, which was the northern port of Antwep, encircle the enemy, and then destroy the disorganized units.

The battle was fought over an 80-mile line from southern Belgium, through the Ardennes Forest, and down to Ettelbruck.

Some of the observers noticed pinpoints of light in the distance as the German artillery fired.

The weather was freezing and the American lay in the wet snow in the winter gear. Many of the soldiers covered their ears, as they waited for the attack, but the shelling continued without interruption. Each second seemed to be an eternity until the invasion. In reality, only an hour passed, before the enemy was engaged.

The anguish and anxiety increased with every individual heartbeat.

Some of the men thought of the possibilities. The strength of the enemy was not known, but all were prepared. Some were calm. Others began to show signs of distress. A few trembled. No one knew what to expect when the battle began.

All were ready to kill or be killed, which was relayed to the various men from their commanders.

The observation posts in the distance relayed messages to their units. These logged structures were of simple construction. One person was in the shelter on a 24-hour basis with rotational shifts. These soldiers along the line were the first to see the invasion and the first to die.

Any noise in the night or day caused nerves to flare. There was always a constant watch. Any dereliction of duty could mean instant death. Binoculars were used to keep a constant vigil. The observers were the first line of defense against the enemy who could attack at any moment.

"Those poor devils," said one of the soldiers in the trench, as he peered into the distance. "Dead meat."

"I was just in one of those observation areas," said Sergeant Messmer.

"We all had our turn," the other soldier said. "Their chances aren't favorable."

The Sergeant laughed and said, "Some have luck and others don't." He placed his finger in his mouth and wet the sight of his rifle. "Let those dirty Krauts come. I can't stand the shelling. Better they come, so we can finish 'um."

"What is against us?" the other soldier asked, as the explosions continued. After rubbing his hands, he continued by saying, "Just too cold."

"We'll know soon enough," said the Sergeant, as he rubbed his eyes. "St. Louis winters were colder." He looked toward the dark sky. "The sun and the Germans will come."

"You from St. Louis, Sarge?" asked one of the soldiers.

"Great place, Private Jefferson," he said. "I lived off of Broadway with my parents by the

Farmers Market in Soulard. There is a nice basketball court in the back on the second floor. Great city."

"I went there once," said the Private. "There is a nice tavern in the city in the wharf district. I don't remember the name. The women were stacked."

"There are many good bars," said the Sergeant. "I visited a few in my 28 years, but mostly in Soulard. In the St Louis heat, a cold beer is necessary. A few good places exist by the riverfront. The area has seen better days."

Another soldier looked toward the sky, before saying, "Too overcast for air support."

The Sergeant looked toward him and then said, "Probably so. Everyone will face the enemy, alone. No choice." He wiped his forehead with his right-gloved hand. "When they come, we will be ready. We have to be. Our position gives us an advantage. As soon as they appear from the fog, we'll have them cold turkey." He paused and then softly stated, "Better than the annoying bombardment."

"I hear the echoes in my head," said another soldier. His name was Jim Conroy. "My brains are being rattled. No time for slumber."

The Sergeant looked toward him and then made the sign of the cross across his chest with his right hand.

The Sergeant was in Company F, 422nd Regiment of the 106th division. There were 4 rifle platoons. Each consisted of 3 squads with about 15 men, per squad. The fourth platoon was the mortar division. There were about 180 men in the Company.

The numbers may have been much greater with over 30 men, per squad. The information varied from certain sources. Memories and data could be corrupted from the time period. For illustration, normal military totals were used for this story, which seem to be more proper. Certain factors from the period may have affected the amount of men for each company and squad.

A Lieutenant was in charge of each platoon. There were 12 squad leaders and 12 assistants. The Staff Sergeant was in charge of the squad. The Sergeant was his assistant, who commanded the corporals, privates, and the others of no rank.

The soldiers of Company F were scattered in trenches and foxholes for about 3/4 of a mile, which was east of the bunkers on a north and south line by the division of the West Wall.

A clearing was in the distance of farmland and a few trees.

The command center with the Captain of the company was in one of the bunkers, which was west of the demarcation line on a hill.

Intelligence was sporadic. There was no air support to confirm any information, which was due to the overcast skies. As the hours continued, the truth would be revealed.

Before the bombardment, one German defector said; an attack would begin at any time. He crossed into American territory with a white flag, and was captured. After being interrogated, the facts were unbelievable, but he could be just a decoy to relay confusion. In any case, there was no time for alterations in the defensive strategies. If the facts were true, nothing could be done.   All the forces were deployed and ready.

Reinforcements were on standby to be deployed for defensive measures.

The men were well trained and time would reveal their destiny.

"Where is Marcus?" asked the Sergeant. "That lazy goof."

"Down the trench to the south," said Corporal Conroy, as he pointed toward him.

"Untrustworthy.   Late for roll call in England," said the Sergeant, "Sleeping it off from a drunken stupor. Our squad had to fill the water buckets for the entire camp."

"He was too tired from his furlough. I have never seen such fine English women. Good drinking."

'That was funny," said the Sergeant, as he chuckled. "Good experience for everyone. He needed the soaking; I gave him. Someday, I'll say that I never knew any of you."

They were in Platoon 2, Squad 3 of Company F.

No one remembered the information. A list with the designations was seen, which may have been destroyed or lost many years ago. The specific numbers may not be correct but are plausible from what was seen on the paperwork.

The other soldier laughed.

"Didn't you tell me of some of your experiences in the States, as an M.P.?" asked Corporal Conroy.

"One time, two of us were escorting a soldier, who was A.W.O.L, back to camp," said the Sergeant. "We all detoured toward a bar for a few cold ones. It was just a little fun. The poor guy deserved one last binge. Well, when we overindulged, the prisoner escaped. He took advantage of our generosity."

"Isn't there a regulation about serving the sentences of escaped prisoners?"

"That's what worried us. We staggered from the bar and began our search. We were too inebriated to really care, but we respected our position and duty. We found him down the street at another bar. After having a few more beers, he was brought back to camp without incident. Nice fellow. He wasn't an enthusiastic draftee. None of us were, but duty should be respected. None of us had any problems with roll call, the next day."

The shelling continued.

"I had a stigmatism," said the Sergeant. "I was supposed to stay in the States. When more men were needed, I was forced to come, like many others."

"What happened to the ones, we replaced?" asked Private Branson. He paused, looked toward the others, and then said, "Don't tell me. I know. Poor devils. I suppose, others are waiting to replace us."

A shell exploded behind their position.

The Sergeant and some of the others smiled, as some dirt, debris, and metal fragments fell on them.

Through radio communications, orders from the Captain came through the ranks, which stated kill or be killed. There was no time for cowards. All had to contribute in order to survive.

The odds were overwhelming.

The enemy was coming and it was a time for killing.

The Staff Sergeant ran toward their position with his rifle in his right hand, as a few shells exploded behind him. "Let the tanks pass," he said. "Concentrate on the infantry. Inform your men."

All nodded in the affirmative, as he departed.

"I'd love taking out one of those babies," said Private Branson.

"You're nuts," said Conroy. "We couldn't even take out one of our tanks."

Another soldier crawled toward the Sergeant in the trench, and then said, "How much longer? Some of the men can't bear the waiting, anymore. The sound is maddening. A few of the younger ones are petrified."

The Sergeant replied, "Just calm down. There's nothing we can do, but fight." He moved toward the other men in the trench to do as the Staff Sergeant commanded. The nerves of some of the others needed to be calmed. He stayed low and then hurried with his Thompson and rifle on his back to the next position.

The Sergeant whispered, as he approached a few men, "When they come, the nightmare will begin."

The men were all different.

There were farmers, merchants, storeowners, clerks, managers, and others of various occupations. Some were shorter and a few were taller. Others were fatter, and a few thinner. Most were Christians of various beliefs. There were men of good morals and others of an unscrupulous nature. All were scared in various ways, but the focus was on survival.

One man, a shopkeeper, was about 48 years old.

They were trained to be a team and given all the skills and tools to help them survive.

Anything could happen. There were no guarantees even with the best training. Bullets and shrapnel have no discrimination. They are random projectiles, which could kill with no regard for anyone.

Various situations were simulated in boot camp. Ropes were climbed. Obstacles were overcome. Rifles and other weapons of destruction were used. Grenades were thrown. The soldiers crawled and marched.

When a few didn't follow orders, accidents did occur.

One time, when the men crawled under barbed wire during training, one of the soldiers was killed. He lifted his head too high. The machine gun fired live rounds, only a few feet above their heads to simulate combat conditions.

The incident was tragic, but remembered. A lesson was learned of disobedience. If orders aren't followed, tragedy results. As the training continued, more discipline was engrained into their souls for the need of a proper command structure.

The training helped prepare the men for battle. A team was created without losing individual initiative. All relied on each other and needed cohesion. The command structure was implanted in their minds with constant discipline.

There were many explosions in their vicinity. Shells impacted the ground and trees. The shelling decreased in the frontal areas, as the enemy advanced. The exact location of each unit was unknown. The noise and unpredictability of the explosions were used, as a preparation of the invasion. Other areas to the rear of their position were more interesting targets for destruction.

Towns, communications, and military targets for the command structure, ammunition, vehicles, and American artillery units were of primary interest to the Germans. The main assault of artillery was not necessary for the individual, except for disorientation.

Even the tanks had their objectives.

No area was sparred the bombardment, but the targets were focused for a better outcome and random for other areas.

Ammunition and gasoline could not be needlessly wasted.

The psychological result of constant bombardment affected American moral and gave the German infantry the best chance for an easy victory.

Three Panzar divisions were ready to attack their sector.

The Captain stayed for the 106th within the pillbox with a few others, which was to the west of Company F. Strategic decisions needed to be formed. Messages from the higher command were received, evaluated, and then relayed through the chain of command. He was totally dedicated to his duty and showed no signs of distress.

Military protocol was followed.

Even when communications were severed, he continued to command with no wavering of his responsibilities. He knew; the entire 106th was under attack from transmissions from St Vith. Information was sporadic during the battle. Everyone was under extreme pressure.

Later, he was ridiculed by many of the troops under his command for staying within the pillbox during the battle. The chain of command could not be sacrificed. The troops were the initial line of defense and his safety was a priority. Without him, the command structure would be severed.

Chaos would result without his leadership.

His death would not serve any purpose. His duty was to command, which was pleasurable. He was a military man and order was needed. His responsibility was to command. The rules were obeyed and nothing caused him to lose focus. His discernment and military experience were vital.

None knew of the overwhelming odds. No enemy was seen and all units concentrated on their sectors. The weather prevented aerial intelligence.

Nothing was seen, except the flashes in the distance, by the observers.

The whistling from the artillery had different sounds.

These noises had a rhythm and meaning to the discernable ears of the soldiers. Certain sounds meant instant death and others were ignored. Each man heard the sounds from their perspective. If one soldier knew he was spared, the death of others was possible.

One of the soldiers saw movement in the distance. He lifted his rifle and fired.

Sergeant Messmer crawled toward his location, and then said, "Don't waste ammunition. They will come, soon enough."

"Sorry, Sarge," the soldier said. "I thought; I saw something."

"You'll know, when they come," said the Sergeant. "Follow training. Make every shot count. Shoot 'um in the chest. Don't waste ammo."

"How many will come?"

"Don't worry, son. We'll handle them. Let any armored vehicles pass through. Our worry is the infantry. Our armored division and artillery will take care of the rest. Mortars will tear 'um to pieces."

"I'm scared, Sarge," the soldier said.

"Boy, how old are you?"

"Eighteen," said the soldier, as he trembled."

"You'll be fine. All of us need each other. None of those Krauts will stand a chance."

The Sergeant removed his gloves, reached into his pocket and then removed a packet of cigarettes. After placing the smoke in his mouth, he offered one to the soldier. "Want one?" he asked, while shaking the container.

The soldier reached for one, as he said, "Thanks."

The pack was returned to the Sergeant's pocket, and then matches ware retrieved. He lit his cigarette and then the one in the boy's mouth. Both puffed. The Sergeant removed it for a few seconds to blow smoke in the air.

The boy coughed from the smoke and then removed the cigarette from his mouth.

"First one," said the Sergeant.

"No," he said, as he continued to cough. "Yes, it is. I don't want it." The boy pushed it into the snow.

"Nasty habit, anyway. Maybe, someday, I'll quit. With the free packs from the commissary, I guess; people are encouraged. A person's right, I suppose. I'd only stop for a good woman."

"You have a dame, Sarge?"

"No steadies. Plenty to choose from back home. They swarm all over me. I'm just not ready. There are too many other priorities," he said, as he glanced into he distance. "Must be attractive to them. I like the attention."

"I wish; I had just one. Something warm to hold."

"We'll both find one, someday. God has everything planned. Too many women just want a good time. A special one is waiting for me. Situations cause change. Do you believe in God, son?"

"I suppose," said the Soldier. "What religion are you?"

"Catholic," he said, as he puffed the cigarette. "Don't attend, as often, as I should. It's just too ceremonial and formal. Some in my family were more religious. They attended every mass. Never could see any difference, but they were good folks. For me, the world had more to offer. Having a good time was more important. Easter and Christmas was always special with the family."

After the Sergeant flicked his cigarette into the distance, he readjusted his helmet, and then placed his gloves on his hands. "The church just seemed too formal and stuffy. Although, I don't know of anything better for a relationship with God."

"Heaven must be a beautiful place."

Mortars landed behind them.

The Sergeant smiled, before saying, "Keep your head down, Ryan. We'll all see heaven, soon enough. I am not planning on dying. We'll both grow old and have stories to tell."

The other soldier smiled.

"Don't think about dying," stated the Sarge. "Death will always come. Life is worth living."

"No, I was just thinking about my dog, Butch."

"Had him long?"

"3 years." Ryan replied.

"My brother and I found a German Shepard, after a tornado in St. Louis. I've never seen, so much destruction. There was debris in the streets. Trees toppled. Brick buildings crumbled." He paused for a few seconds, smiled, and then continued, "I believe that the year was 1929 in the spring. That animal was vicious. A police dog, probably. We tried to keep it, but my parents wouldn't stand for it. We gave it to one of my Uncles, who owned a store. That animal was very protective and loyal to him. Maybe, he knew how to handle him. Great guard dog."

"Butch isn't mean. We had fun, together. She seemed to understand my every word."

"What kind of dog?"

"A golden retriever."

"Just keep your head down, and aim for the chest," said the Sergeant, as he slapped the top of his helmet.

A smile was on the soldiers face.

The Sergeant crawled from him, as the shelling continued.

Tanks, mortars, and the big guns continually fired. Shells were loaded into the weapons. The area was pounded for an hour without hesitation. No one thought silence would return, but each man knew, if silence returned, even for a brief period, the Germans were ready to begin their offensive.

The Germans were confident of their plan to split the American and British forces. They would be easily trapped and squeezed, until every one of the allies were defeated.

Their German soldiers were ready for the attack but many were weary from previous campaigns. The wondered when they could return victorious to their homeland. The glory was diminished from the early years of the war.

This battle brought smiles on many of their faces and a new hope.

Hitler wanted to bring a victory and pride to his men. No one could defeat the Third Reich. They were the master race and superior to everyone. All would submit to their will. He needed his power and status established.

When Hitler heard the word, Ardennes, he slapped his hand on a desk, and gave the order, months earlier, to prepare for their greatest battle.

If they could break the back of the British and American forces, Europe would be under their reign. A new order would be established.

Hitler's legacy would be firmly planted in the memories of the conquered. All would submit or die. No one would escape his wrath. Power and greed was motivated by a disturbed mentality.

The men of Company F knew nothing of the motives and tyranny of Adolph Hitler.

The concentration camps for the Jews, Christians, and those with darker skin were hidden in Poland, Germany and other areas. Their purpose was concealed from the masses. Anyone, who complained of Hitler's leadership, was killed. Others disappeared. The leadership of the Third Reich encouraged the genocide, while others ignored it. All submitted to the will of their leader, even if some thought; he was deranged.

Many benefited from his reign. Profit was their motive, so they glorified his position, until he wasn't needed. Many respected him, but others thought; he was a madman. The ones, who weren't needed, were destroyed. All their property and wealth was transferred to the Nazis to sustain their positions.

To the common German soldier, they obeyed orders. They had nothing to do with the politics of the moment. Many were proud and other loyal, but the ranks were growing wearier of their purpose. The allies were decimating their homeland with no hope for victory.

This campaign increased their hopes.

For the ones, who died, they must win. Too many of their people suffered. While Hitler was their leader, rules were obeyed. The soldiers all knew; he needed a glorious victory to increase the pride of the Fatherland. All were ready for the battle. The power and might of their military strength would survive in many of their thoughts.

Others knew their reach for power was being overextended.

Whether someone was Christian, Jewish, black, white, atheist, or of a certain nationality, all blood was red. Death brought pain to all. All were created in God's image. Self or God was the factor, which caused a person to obey the needs of the flesh or of a higher power. The love of man was not the love of God.

The differences couldn't be understood by anyone without discernment from a higher realm.

Each weapon continued its terror during the first hour. The men loaded and fired within clear guidelines of their targets. Smoke billowed from the German tanks, canons, and mortars. The Germans artillery was overpowering. Their ammunition was endless. The precision of the process was seamless.

Some Americans and British soldiers were wounded and others killed during the attack.

Certain targets were of primary concern to the Germans. Other areas were randomly attacked to increase fear and anxiety. Towns and military objectives were easier to destroy. The infantry needed to attack the enemy with all their strength. None of the German missiles had enough power to eliminate the threat of the enemy. Direct confrontation was the only option.

When needed the more powerful weapons could help stop the resistance, quickly.

The mission was to confuse the enemy. Communication within the command structure needed to be severed. Ammunition exhausted. Supply lines broken. Moral of their enemy reduced.

The Germans were on the offensive, while their opponents were defending a worthless cause. Their enemy's spirit needed to be crushed. Their will diminished. This battle was a return to glory for the Fatherland, which would ignite a new hope and a better tomorrow.

The commanders engrained the exuberance into their men. Most were convinced; an easy victory awaited them. None of the allies knew of the massiveness of their forces and power of their weapons. The positive nature was contagious, which alleviated most of the fears of the pending conflict.

The one miscalculation was the determination of a free people and the endless stream of recruits, who would never relent, until the battle was won to break the chains of tyranny.

Suddenly, the shelling at the front lines decreased.

The frontal observers reported, an unbelievable sight, as daylight was seen on the horizon. The German forces were massive. Countless tanks and soldiers were approaching. The sight was unbelievable.

"My God!" one of the observers yelled, before one of the tanks fired rounds into his position, which killed him.

All communications from St Vith, the outposts, and other areas were eventually silenced, as the German's advanced toward the Siegfried Line.

The personal confrontation began.

Chapter Two: The First Day

The silence, before the bombardment, brought peaceful sensations. Now, the experience changed. All knew the momentary quietness was a warning. The enemy was approaching. The battle was ready to begin with a face-to-face confrontation. The calmness was more frightening. All focused their attention toward the incoming forces.

As the sun rose, the blood and debris was visible on the landscape.

Some of the soldiers within the 106th Division were wounded. A few were killed. If the wounds weren't serious, the men stayed to fight, while others were transported to aid stations. The dead were moved to other locations, or left in their position.

Medics were overwhelmed.

Thousands of Germans wore white uniforms and walked behind the tanks across the front. The noise of the approaching vehicles slowly increased. Weapons were pointed toward the Americans.

The Germans were ready and confident.

"They're coming," said Sergeant Messmer, as he heard the tanks in the distance. "Ready weapons!"

Staff Sergeant Waller looked in various directions, and then said, "Keep your heads down! Don't engage the tanks! Target the infantry!"

The mortar division of the 4th Platoon began to fire into the distance. Their squads were placed in strategic locations, which benefited the other men. Shells were loaded and the projectiles were launched toward the opposing forces. The men fired in rapid succession.

Explosions from mortars pounded the clearings from the American positions on the Siegfried Line.

The Sergeant stated, "The path for the tanks is limited."

"The trees wouldn't stop them," the Staff Sergeant said. "We're not their priority. The infantry is our concern. The mortars should hold back their troops for the moment."

The noise of a tank was heard approaching their position within the fog. Only shadows were visible. The sound increased, as it appeared about 100 feet in the distance and then began to roll toward them.

As the tank continued, snow was pushed to the side of the threads.

"Hold your fire!" the Staff Sergeant exclaimed. The noise increased, before he said, "Let it pass in the clearing between the trees."

If the tanks had no access through the forest, the vehicles turned, before reaching the trench, which was behind a hedgerow. Roads and clearings were used to proceed toward more vital targets. Some of the tanks fired rounds, but the ammunition wasn't wasted on the infantry.

Memories flashed within the Sergeants thoughts.

He began to think of his family. They gave him love. Respect for others was engrained within his inner core, since early childhood. The threads of honesty and integrity were the moral standards of his parents.

People, who stole from others, have always upset him.

None of his parents, brothers, and sisters was perfect. They had a love for everyone but their demeanor lacked substance. Nothing glowed from within their core. All were good people. Something was missing even if love was demonstrated.

Understanding was lacking.

While he was an MP, a couple of his responsibilities were to guard and feed the German Prisoners in the States. He was required to bring food into their common area. He was cautious. Although weary from the fight, these men were dangerous and capable of causing problems.

A gun was always in his holster.

Before entering the cell, he removed the bullets to prevent problems. Experiences from other guards were a factor. Stories were known of incidents with the prisoners. No one suspected his deception. The Germans respected his authority and the weapon.

Thick steaks and potatoes satisfied the hunger of the German prisoners. Cultural standards were used to feed different nationalities. Diets were consistent with their normal routines. These accommodations were necessary to satisfy everyone's desires.

There were many German prison camps in the states. The Germans under his responsibility were well treated and respected. The authorities authorized no abuse of the captives. Although they were treated and feed well, life in a foreign land was unbearable.

For some of the captives, their will to fight was not broken.

The Sergeant focused on the enemy and the hazards during the battle.

The machine gun on the tank began to fire, as it rolled past them.

The grinding noise of the motors intensified.

"Fire!" yelled the Staff Sergeant, as Germans appeared from the fog. "Kill or be killed!"

Both sides began the assault. Some of the Germans fired in a standing position. Others found cover behind a few trees and other debris within the field. A few of the Germans fell to the ground, while the mortars fell within their ranks. Machine guns and bazookas were quickly used against the American forces.

The Americans fought back with vigor.

Bullets penetrated flesh. Blood gushed from the impacts and puddles of red covered the snow. Bodies flew in the air. Limbs were severed. Men became human torches.

A few American soldiers were too scared to fire, while most performed with distinction. Some vomited, while others violently shook, until they needed to fight. Others showed no mercy toward the enemy.

Chances were taken, which resulted in death. As the battle raged, emotions increased with everyone. Men sacrificed themselves with daring maneuvers to protect their positions. If a soldier thought no hope existed, he fought with vigor to kill the enemy.

Survival was the only option.

The dying cried for help, as the battle raged.

As the mortars fell within the incoming forces and other weapons used, most of the wounded Germans were killed. Only the soldiers, who threatened their defensive position, were targeted. None of the fallen or wounded was deliberately killed, unless they continued to fight.

A few of the Germans ran from the battle and many of them were shot or killed from shrapnel.

The Sergeant tired something that he saw in a movie. He made gobbling sounds, which cause a few of the Germans to be too inquisitive. After aiming carefully, he killed each one of them with his rifle. Blood splattered from their bodies as they fell backwards.

The air was so cold that the pools of blood immediately froze.

"Master race," whispered the Sergeant, sarcastically. "They bleed, like everyone else."

The entire 106th division was engaged with the enemy.

"Sarge," said Corporal Conroy with disbelief. "A few are just old men and kids."

"Keep firing," he said, "It's them or us!"

Other Germans retreated into the fog.

Grenades were thrown from both sides.

Staff Sergeant Waller shouted, "Kill them! All the Krauts must die!"

Grenades exploded all around their position.

One landed by the Sergeant's head.

After lowering his head, he waited for the explosion. The few seconds seemed like an eternity. He knew his head would be blown off but nothing happened.

Sergeant Messmer slowly raised his head. For a few seconds, he frightfully stared toward the grenade, before throwing it into the distance. Relief was apparent with his facial expressions.

Both sides continued the battle for hours. The intensity varied at certain intervals. Both sides learned from their mistakes and tried to overwhelm their opponents. The Germans dug in but as more were killed more arrived to continue the fight.

Casualties were mounding for the Americans.

A First Lieutenant in the 589th field artillery held his position for a sustained period on December 16 under heavy mortar and artillery fire. The area was under constant attack. His men continued to fire upon the enemy under constant bombardment. Certain targets were assigned and the artillery was used to destroy enemy positions.

As orders were received, the First Lieutenant ran to each placement. All the men were informed of the next target. Mortar and other weapons fire were occurring toward their position. Without regard for safety, he continued to relay the commands.   As the defensive artillery was fired, the men held their positions. His courage motivated his men to continue the assault on incoming forces.

Three Infantry units and Nazi tanks were approaching.

"Target the enemy!" the First Lieutenant screamed.

The guns were aimed toward the opposition.

He continued by shouting, "Take careful aim! Fire for effect! Fire!"

The First Lieutenant continued to move from one artillery position to another.   Orders were given and the guns adjusted.   As their position was continually being shelled, their weapons fired upon the advancing German troops and the tanks. Explosions were seen in the distance between the advancing forces.

One tank was destroyed and the enemy retreated under intense American fire.

The First Lieutenant was ordered to move his battery through Schonberg. German troops and tanks entered the town. He continued to run between the guns to direct fire, until only one artillery piece remained. The unit was hit and two men were killed.

The Lieutenant was the last to evacuate. As the Krauts chased him, he departed on the road. On occasion, he turned and fired toward the oncoming forces. The enemy returned fire. Even after being shot, he was relentless. He avoided their aggression to the best of his ability. The Germans were in pursuit. With his weakened condition, all the men finally were within close proximity.

All began to fire toward each other.

No one saw the Lieutenant, until his body was found near Myrode, Belgium with five dead Germans around him. After withdrawing from the town, he was finally killed by advancing forces. If the only outcome was death, the only choice was to kill the enemy with determination.

The 106th needed reinforcements and more ammunition. Communications were severed with headquarters and the other divisions.

They were cut off with no hope of salvation.

Chaos was everywhere.

Another soldier in the 634th was moving his machine gun to a more defensive position. The Americans were under extreme fire from the Germans. He volunteered to stay while the others continued to withdraw. As he repositioned the machine gun, he began to fire.

"Die, you stinking Krauts!" screamed a Private.

Tanks and enemy troops were approaching. The Germans focused their attention toward him. The bullets and explosions around him didn't decrease his vigor. He intensely fired upon the enemy, which caused them to postpone their advance.

When a tank approached, the Private continued to fire.

"Burn to hell!" the Private shouted, as he continued to fire.

The tank had a 88mm gun, which fired upon his position. Bullets impacted the area. He had no chance and was killed. Although the German soldiers lost many men, they were relieved and gratified, when the obstacle was neutralized.

With the enemy's diversion from their objective, many other lives were spared. The delay helped with the redeployment of American troops. Although the battle continued, the Private knew the risks of his decision. His death gave others a chance to survive until the next encounter with the enemy.

Another Lieutenant in the 424th with his 3 platoons was under extreme artillery attack. The shelling was intense. The explosions caused many men to cover their heads and ears with their arms. As each bomb impacted their position, dirt and debris flew into the air and impacted around them. The men stayed low in the trench. After the shelling decreased, all eyes were directed toward the incoming forces. The number of enemy troops was massive and all the men were shocked.

With no regard for his safely the Lieutenant moved toward various positions and fired. As he exposed himself to enemy fire, his men were astonished. The tactic exposed the Germans, which caused them to be easy targets. The men waited, carefully aimed, and then fired toward the Germans with precision. Enough of the enemy was killed, which allowed the American troops to retreat.

During the repositioning of his troops, the Lieutenant was killed.

Explosions and gunfire occurred down the entire front of Company F and other areas. The intensity of the battle was worse than the initial shelling. The noise was deafening. The sounds echoed through countryside.

More Germans were killed. Some fell backwards and became lifeless. Others staggered, before they dropped. Others cried for help, before dying. A few shook, violently, and screamed, before no more movement was seen.

Bodies were everywhere.

The Americans were relentless with their defensive measures. Some of the valiant American squads were overwhelmed. Others were evenly matched, as the enemy continued to push toward them. Most men continued to hold the defensive positions for the moment.

"We've had it!" exclaimed one of the American soldiers. "They're everywhere!" Just like locusts."

"Keep firing!" shouted the Lieutenant, as a mortar exploded, behind his position. "We'll hold 'um!"

All types of weapons were used on both sides. Smoke filled the air. Bullets impacted the men on both sides. Bodies and body parts flew into the air. Bazookas were aimed and fired. Mortars flew in the air toward their targets. Shrapnel flew in various directions. Anyone in the destructive past of these projectiles was killed, injured, or marred.

Bullets and pieces of metal impacted the ground, the trees, and ricocheted from boulders.

One grenade after another was thrown toward the enemy. Bodies flew into the air. Trees were shattered. Vehicles exploded. Arms, heads, and other body parts flew into he air.

The enemy was relentless with the attack.

One soldier after another dropped from the bullets and explosions. Some of them became living torches, until they dropped into the snow.

The fires continued, as their bodies became cinders.

The Germans used the dead, and the wounded, as shields. More bullets impacted the fallen. There was really no time to help anyone but a few dragged themselves to safety. Some of their comrades dragged others away from the hellish experience.

The cycle of death continued until corpses were everywhere.

This was a time of killing.

"Die, you scum!" said another soldier, as he fired his B.A.R. Bullets impacted around his position, as he continued to fire his weapon.

Explosion after explosion was seen from the pillbox, which was west of the fighting on the hill. The men were fighting bravely. Their positions were being held for most of the day. The enemy continued their relentless assault into the afternoon and evening in certain areas.

Smoke filled the air.

The smell of death was blown with the smoke and cinders. Death was everywhere. No one escaped the hell of war. A living nightmare became a reality.

Staff Sergeant Browski grabbed the radio, and then exclaimed, "Able Baker, I need the Lieutenant, now! This is Sergeant Browksi. Give me the Lieutenant!" Bomb exploded around his position. Projectiles flew past his head.

The Lieutenant responded by asking, "What's the situation?"

"In the name of God, help us!"

"There is no help!" Lieutenant Masters shouted. "Make do. Do you hear me? Make do! The entire line is being hit. Communications are down. If other squads contain their area, we'll send help. The Captain wants you to hold the line! Kill as many, as you can. Reinforcements were requested. Nothing else is available." After a brief silence, he asked, "What's the status of the ammo?"

"Being depleted."

"Use what you have. Hold off, as long as possible, before withdrawing. Give them everything; you have. Do you hear me?"

"Yes, Lieutenant," he said. "Understood. Over and out." He turned off the radio, before saying, "What do they expect?"

"When we're dead, nothing more," replied another soldier.

The offensive of the Germans caused casualties in many areas. With the 592d field artillery, the result was the same. Many men were wounded and needed help, while the Germans advanced and attacked. None of the American forces could move forward to retrieve the wounded.

A Captain risked his life by constantly pulling men to safety under enemy fire. One man was dragged about 40 yards. The fighting was intense but he continued to retrieve the wounded without regard for his own safety. As bullets were fired toward him, he was relentless with the recovery of the men, who needed immediate medical attention.

After the battery was reorganized, the fighting continued. Until darkness, the enemy was held back. As the Americans retreated, heavy shelling overwhelmed the convoy. Some trucks were damaged and men were wounded.

Even under these circumstances, the Captain continued to help the men in need. Some of them couldn't be moved. The Captain had no choice but to order the undamaged trucks to leave him with the injured men. The wounded were the priority. No other choice existed.

The risk was known within everyone's thoughts.

"You'll be fine!" shouted the Captain toward the injured men. "Just hold on, until the medics arrive." He tried to attend to their needs. "No need to worry. Help in on the way."

He knew their chances were slim. All were exposed to enemy fire. The Germans were advancing. Whether the Germans would kill all of item or attend to their needs was not known. With everything in chaos, the chance of rescue wasn't plausible by medical personnel.

The remained men in the convoy never knew what happened to the Captain and the others, after leaving them on the road. All may have been taken prisoner or killed by the advancing German forces. The preceding haunted their thoughts. The courage of their commander always was remembered. Their leader was an inspiration for his sacrifice.

A company from the 424th was pinned down in another area, which prevented their advancement. German machine guns and small arms fire were aimed toward their position. The soldiers were in a desperate situation. The opposition had the advantage.

Escape seemed impossible.

"I need options," said First Sergeant Grayson.

"Without help, we have no chance," Corporal Maxwell stated. "Maybe, with mortars and artillery."

"We'll all be killed, if we don't act. Those Krauts are well dug in. Something must be done, before they're reinforced."

The chess game continued.

The forces exchanged fire. Periods of time elapsed when nothing occurred. The Germans had the advantage. At any time, more troops could arrive with more powerful weapons. Before the odds increased for the Germans, the Americans needed to act.

With courage, the First Sergeant stood and began to charge toward the enemy. The men were amazed at his actions. Cover fire was supplied. While advancing, he was under heavy weapons fire. One by one the men raised themselves from their positions and followed his actions. All of them began to scream and continue to fire their weapons toward the enemy.

All the Germans were stunned.

Many stared toward the Americans with amazement, as they fired. None expected such a bold maneuver. Weapons were continually fired toward all the incoming forces. The flashes from the guns were menacing, as both sides continued the assault. Nothing deterred the Americans, as the Germans were astonished with the unexpected assault.

All of the Germans were killed with some fatalities and other injuries to the American forces.

With the unpredicted action of the First Sergeant, the enemy in their sector was defeated. The Germans were surprised and unable to properly respond. Their position couldn't be defended from the suicidal charge. Since the Germans expected an easy victory, the action was a total surprise to their rules of conduct.

Company F was spread out over a wide area in pockets. The Germans hit all areas hard. As more Germans fell, machine guns were used to pin down the squads. Until reinforcements, arrived, the German soldiers were redeployed. Certain areas needed more attention.

The horror continued.

The Captain stayed within the pillbox and tried with a few others to organize a plan of action.

The situation was still controllable but casualties were mounting. He received messages from the various squads, who desperately needed help. There was nothing; he could do. The severity of the situation was not known from the other divisions. The lines of communication were severed.

Most of his men were holding their defensive positions.

"The Captain just stays in his bunker," said Staff Sergeant Barker. "We're defending him, like a scared cow."

"Rank has privileges," said a Corporal.

"Just shut up," he stated. "Dragging him into hell would be pleasurable." The Staff Sergeant looked to his right and observed the bloody body of his Sergeant lying in the snow.

His head was a few feet from him.

In the bunker, Captain Grant talked to a couple of his Lieutenants.

"Any suggestions?" he asked.

One of the Lieutenants answered, and said, "Dead bodies cover the landscape. Our men are fighting with bravery. Our casualties are increasing, but we're holding them. Their force is just too overwhelming. The more we kill, the more eventually come."

"Ammunition is the major problem," said the other Lieutenant. "Most squads are still pinned down. The situation is desperate."

"I don't want excuses!" he yelled. "Hold the line until the men can safely retreat to higher ground. Take ammo from the dead. Send a squad out on recon patrol. We need more information."

"A few squads have been decimated. The survivors were seen being pushed by the Germans toward St. Vith. Regrouping with other units may be beneficial. A couple of the other squads have retreated toward the ridgeline. They're spread out for about a mile."

"We need as much information, as possible," said the Captain. "Give me options."

One of Lieutenants saluted and left the bunker, while the other asked, "The Germans are deliberately depleting our ammo."

"With the sacrifice of their men," said the Captain, as he walked toward a map on the table and then pointed toward it. "With one of the last communications, I was told that the entire front is being attacked." He placed his finger on the surface of the paper. "We are here. Most likely, their forces will be diverted to other areas, as our threat diminishes." After briefly turning his head toward the Lieutenant, he continued by saying, "Only a small contingent is needed to hold our troops until the ammo is exhausted and the moral is shot to hell. Without support, our ability to fight will be exhausted. Machine gun nests will be keep us contained. Inform all the squads to retreat toward to the ridgeline. If they can hold, wait until dark. Safest alternative."

The Lieutenant reluctantly said, "All will continue the fight on higher ground and pray for help."

An explosion occurred outside the bunker.

Dust fell into the room, before the Captain stated, "In the face of adversity, bravery arises."

"All deserve medals for their bravery," said the Lieutenant.

"No one gets anything from me for doing their job. My men fight to survive. There is no honor in war."

"Holding the hill will be difficult."

The Captain turned toward him, and then said, "When more information is obtained, the correct decision will be relayed to the men. He paused, before continuing his words, "If reinforcements and necessary supplies arrive in time, we'll kick their butts to hell. Without communication, we know nothing of the condition of the other areas. The towns and military targets were probably hit hard. We can only count on our initiative to survive. Let all pray for help. For now, we are cut off and alone."

"On another matter, a few of the young men deserted during the bombardment."

"Bunch of wimps," said the Captain. "The Germans will have easy targets with those cowards. Should have shot them on the run."

"They just cracked under the pressure," stated the Lieutenant.

"No excuses. They should have died with honor and not by disgracing my Company."

Both stared toward each other and then looked toward the map.

Bullets and mortars continued to impact the Americans position.

The intensity decreased but the situation was still hazardous. The Germans set up machine gun nests at various intervals. Their objective was to contain the American forces. Any visible movement caused a response. Easy access was their advantage to supplies and reinforcements.

The moral of the Americans forces was declining.

Ammunition was at dangerous levels but enough was available to sustain them for the moment. Many of the soldiers were wounded or killed. Most of the ones, who were injured, stayed in the trench, but some were reached by the medics and treated. A few were taken toward the ridgeline for further evaluation.

There was no need to move the dead.

Another soldier crawled toward, Sergeant Messmer's position, and said, "Lester and Cole are dead."

"Ryan Lester?" asked the Sergeant.

"Yes, he took one in the head."

The Sergeant frowned, before saying, "We'll hold him." He rubbed his face, which showed signs of distress. The sounds of the bombardment echoed through his mind. His focus was on the enemy but any deaths to his men increased his anxiety and sorrow.

The soldier departed.

The Staff Sergeant crawled toward the Sergeant, and then said, "John, that machine gun nest must be neutralized. Other squads have the same problem. Retreating in the darkness may be their only option. If we don't pull back to the hill, we'll all be surrounded and killed. The Germans have broken through to the left flank. We have orders from the Lieutenant to withdraw. Any options?"

"Crawling through the drainage ditch may be beneficial," Sergeant Messmer replied, as he pointed toward the right. "It goes close to their position. We can do it. Any grenades?"

The Staff Sergeant replied, "A couple."

"We can do it," he confidently said. "The fog will help. Who do you want to send? Let's show the youngsters how it's done."

"Risky but possible," started the Staff Sergeant. "This job does require experience. We'll spare the young ones the hardship."

The Sergeant stared toward him. He said nothing, but the expression on his face showed more anxiety, even if he thought; the plan was necessary.

"No other options. None of us will stand a chance in hell, otherwise. The men can open up and give us cover. The crossfire will force them to make quick decisions and fatal mistakes. The element of surprise works both ways."

"We'll take 'um," the Sergeant said, as he smiled.

"If they become complacent, they will become easy targets. While they're occupied with our squad, we will position ourselves. We'll wait for the right moment and then I will throw a grenade. If they show themselves, open fire."

They talked for a period of time to discuss their options and safety concerns.

"Should I inform the others?" asked the Sergeant, as he affixed his bayonet to his rifle.

The Staff Sergeant looked toward him with curiosity and bewilderment.

"Protocol," stated the Sergeant. "Always be prepared."

"Sounds like suicide to me," said Corporal Conroy.

"No," said the Staff Sergeant, as he glanced toward the Corporal. "You just volunteered."

He responded, "Lucky me."

"Just tell the others to give us cover," said the Sergeant.

"We may not hit anything," the soldier said. "They have a good position at the edge of the clearing. They're veiled within the fog."

The Sergeant smiled, before saying, "Just be a distraction. We have to do something, before the fog clears. Visibility is improving. We need the advantage, before others arrive and all of us are killed."

"Tell them, when we're in position, to open fire," said the Staff Sergeant, as the Corporal crawled from them. "If we're spotted, give them hell. Watch out for other Krauts."

The Staff Sergeant turned his head toward the Sergeant. "You're a disgrace," he stated. "Just look at your coat. It's shredded and full of holes. A guardian angel must be protecting you. You alright?"

He chuckled, before saying, "Never felt better," After observing his appearance, he continued, "Ventilated." He glanced toward the dead men around his position. "Others were more worthy."

"All have a time to die."

"Maybe so," said the Sergeant. "The coat was too big, anyway. I'll requisition a new one." After realizing what could have happened, he began to slightly shake, and then he softly stated, "Just a whisper from death."

The Sergeant placed his hand over his ears, as the sound of the explosions continued within him.

Prisoners were being taken from many sectors.

Soldiers were separated from their units. Others were too scared to fight and just needed an escape from the violence. No one could hide anywhere. The Germans were advancing. Their tanks from various sectors advanced 9 miles to the west of the Siegfried Line. More infantry penetrated the lines, as defenses collapsed. Many of the American soldiers from various sectors were killed and others surrendered.

All were negatively affected by the ordeal both physically and mentally.

About 23,000 of the American forces were captured; about 47,500 were wounded, and about 19,000 were killed over the course of the entire battle. The estimates vary between 60,000 to 100,000, who were captured, wounded, killed, and missing.

The exact figures may never be known.

"You ready?" asked Staff Sergeant Waller.

"Let's take 'um," the Sergeant replied.

Both men began to crawl through the gully to outflank the enemy.

The remaining members of the squad were prepared and ready.

Both sides had a relentless spirit for their cause. As men fell, the fighting became more personal. There was no time to think of death as the battle raged but the quiet moments brought contemplation of purpose. All concentrated on their goals. The fight was for survival. The ones, who died, had no more pain.

All worries ended with death.

The fallen just lay where they were wounded. Some were sprawled on the snow and others lay in the trench. The battle raged around them. Cries for help through the fog were heard from some. Others cried, no more. Frozen puddles of blood were around many of the injured. As their energy of life decreased, the horrors of the battle seemed meaningless.

The sounds faded from their senses as the injured began to die.

The medics administered first aid. Even under enemy fire, they performed their duties with honor. They treated the sick and helped many to safety. Although some were also wounded and others killed, none of the others were deterred.

Other soldiers helped their friends and brothers.

Many used sulfur on their wounds, until help arrived, as they lay in the snow, trench, or foxhole. Some of the wounds were superficial and didn't require immediate medical attention.

Many of the injured continued to fight.

Sergeant Messmer and Staff Sergeant Waller removed their packs and began to crawl within the gully toward the north of the machine gun nest. Gunfire and explosions were heard from many directions, which masked any noise. The distance was hazardous but the ditch kept them hidden.

The Germans didn't fire, unless movement was seen. They kept a constant vigil on the American position. Their viewpoint gave them a clear line of fire and better visibility from the sunlight. If any of the Americans tried retreat, they would be instantly killed.

Those rounds could tear anyone into pieces.

Complacency was their weakness.

They didn't know the terrain and maybe the machine gun nest wasn't placed in a defensible position. Haste was used instead of judgment. Confidence was within them but time affected their senses. The Germans expected anything, but they knew; there was no chance of escape for the enemy.

The squad was in a desperate situation.

When reinforcements arrived, the Germans would have an easy kill.

The two noncommissioned officers continued to crawl toward their objective.

Their squad waited and watched for the proper moment. Timing was critical. Their lives depended on the outcome. All were ready to create the diversion.

"We'll get 'um." said the Sergeant in a low tone, as he crawled behind him. "Everyone will be killed, if we don't act."

"The element of surprise," the Staff Sergeant whispered, as he briefly turned his head toward him.

Bombs exploded in the distance and intense gunfire was heard.

The Sergeant softly laughed, and said, "They won't stand a chance."

"Always be proud of our squad. They fought with honor."

"Good men," said the Sergeant, "even if they are goof offs. Too many families will mourn, today. Maybe, we'll give our men a chance to live."

The men's faces were dirty from the smoke. All were weary from the fight. None knew, if the plan would succeed. The courage; they saw gave them strength. Hope was within them as much as desperation. The outcome would determine their fate.

"The Sarge is trying to save our necks," one of them of the squad members said.

"Stan, two of us should be out there."

"He always protected us," said the first man. "All of us were like sons to him, Mel.

"Mother hen, sometimes," said a third soldier. "Both are fools. Just be ready."

"Maybe, just overprotective," said Mel Stone. "Ron, just be ready."

"He'll have stories to tell his wife and family, someday," said the first man."

"If he survives," said Ron. "No one will remember, this day, if none survive. Who'd want to remember? He glanced toward his rifle, and then said, "In heaven, if I see any Germans, who I personally killed, I'd apologize."

"You may not have long to wait," stated Stan, as he smiled.

The men continued to crawl and were almost in position.

"We need a better position," whispered the Staff Sergeant. "Not good. The fog won't help us. We'll have to crawl out the ditch. He paused, before saying, "Behind those bushes by the fallen tree trunk." He pointed into the distance. "If they are surprised, they may become easy targets. If they spot us, open up. Get in that depression, over there. Better line of fire. I'll try to throw a grenade or two at the proper moment. When the men open up, run with all your strength. Give me cover."

As they crawled past a dead German soldier, the Sergeant glanced toward his weapons, and whispered, "Good thing that grenade didn't go off. My head would have been blown off."

"What did you say?" the Staff Sergeant quietly asked.

"Defective equipment."

The Staff Sergeant said, "Our grenades better work." He lifted his head and noticed the two Germans with the machine gun about 50 feet to the right. "Hitler is a madman."

"They're old enough to kill," the Sergeant said.

They crawled a few more yards and the firing from their men began.

After a few more seconds, the Staff Sergeant began to crawl from the ditch, "Let's go," he softly said.

"Be careful," said Sergeant Messmer. "Keep your head down."

Both exited the ditch, as one of the German soldiers noticed the men toward his right.

"Ameracana!" yelled one of the Germans. "Ameracana!" He pointed toward them.

The machine gun was turned. The area was sprayed with bullets. Before the Staff Sergeant was killed, he threw a grenade, which fell short. The Sergeant lay on the ground, as if he was dead, after a few rounds hit around him. The Germans saw no signs of movement. Both were satisfied; the Americans were dead.

The threat was eliminated.

"Both are down!" yelled some of the squad. "Keep firing!"

"They're dead!" yelled another soldier, as he repeatedly fired his rifle. "Stinking Krauts! The Sarge is dead! They're both dead."

The machine gun was again turned toward their position.

It continued to fire toward them, as the Germans smiled. The men hid themselves in the trench as bullets impacted the trees and ground. Bark flew from the trees and dirt flew in the air.

"What are we going to do, now?" asked Little Joe Banner.

"Stop firing!" shouted Bob Bert. "Save ammo! We'll wait until darkness and try to pull back." He hit the snow with his left hand.

All were helpless.

The Germans ceased firing and continued to smile. They turned toward the men, who tried to kill them, but no movement was seen. Both were motionless.

The Americans were killed and no longer a threat. They felt proud of their accomplishment.

The Sergeant lay motionless.

He wasn't injured. The bullets just missed him. One twitch or sneeze could be disastrous. Playing dead was the only option. If they became complacent, he could act.

One eye was carefully opened at various intervals for about 30 minutes.

He saw them laughing. They even had coffee and a few cigarettes. He waited for the right moment to do something. Killing others was a pleasure to them. Neither had any morality.

The machine gun was fired at various intervals toward his men.

He couldn't think, properly. His mind was spinning. Thoughts were confused. Everything seemed surreal. He was scared and petrified at the possibilities.

Noises were in the background and within him. He couldn't escape the horror. All he could hear was the bullets and explosions from the past and the ones in the distance. His thoughts of the horror were prevalent.

The squad needed him. They had no escape, if he did nothing.

Fear overwhelmed him, as he stayed motionless, but he was the only hope.

The Germans continued to fire a few rounds toward the squad to remind them of their fate. Mostly, the Germans relaxed and were confident of their superiority, which overwhelmed their senses.

Attention was removed from the Sergeant's position. His presence was forgotten. The time to act was now. He reached for his rifle. Hesitation was within his thoughts, but he needed to eliminate the enemy.

Rising from the dead was his only option. He knew what needed to be done. Fear was suppressed. He wasn't deterred and was ready.

He quickly lifted himself and ran as fast as he could toward their position.

"Ameracana!" shouted one of the Germans.

As one squad member saw movement though the fog, he shouted, "It's the Sarge! He's alive!" He aimed his rifle.

"Hold your fire, Carl!" shouted Little Joe. "You'll hit him!"

"Get them, Sarge!" he shouted. "Blood and guts!"

The machine gun was turned toward him but it jammed. The other tried to pull his revolver, as the Sergeant quickly approached their position through the snow.

He raised his rifle and then rifle butted the German with the pistol.

The Sergeant then turned his rifle toward the other one and bayoneted him in the chest, as both stood face to face. The German's expression was horrifying. His body became stiff for a moment as his white uniform became soaked with blood. The Sergeant pulled the bayonet from the man's chest and then the German fell to the ground.

The squad stood and cheered as the Sergeant gave them the thumbs up sign.

No other emotions were seen as the Sergeant momentarily stared toward the body of his friend, the Staff Sergeant.

He quickly returned to his men, and then yelled, "Let's get out of here. Grab your gear! Move it!"

There was no time for mourning. Ammunition, weapons, and supplied were gathered. All of the men evacuated to higher ground. Their position was evacuated. The memories were engrained within all of them.

During the battle about half of Company F were killed or injured.

All the men fought bravely. They were in a hopeless situation. Training only gave them the basics. They fought for survival from a basis instinct.

The experience was engrained into their souls. The horror never escaped the survivors and many needed counseling after the war. Others were shell-shocked and eventually blocked the ordeal. A few never could escape their memories. All were scared for life. The past haunted all of them, until they eventually died.

The Germans suffered more wounded and casualties, as they continued to advance and were shredded to pieces. Hundreds were killed in the vicinity of Company F. They just lay were they fell. A time for mourning was past.

The living continued the fight.

During the entire Battle of the Bulge, over 15,000 Germans were killed, over 41,000 wounded, and over 27,000 were captured or missing in action.

Chapter Three: The Hill

The men either died or retreated. No other options existed. Some squads fought longer than others as they were pushed back. A few retreated to different areas, as the German forces overwhelmed them.

Most squads found higher ground to have a better defensive position.

Death was everywhere. Towns were still being shelled. American tanks and artillery positions were being decimated by the massive attack of the Third Reich. The push continued, which caused massive destruction for the American and British forces.

Casualties and injuries increased.

Reinforcements were diverted from other areas to stop the German advance.

More Information was needed to properly plan for a counteroffensive. The attack was a surprise to the allies. Nothing substantial was known of the massive nature of the invasion. Time was of the essence.

Everyone was stunned.

Strategies were discussed. Preparations began to stop their advance. Troops and other equipment were being assembled. The defeat of the German forces was the only priority in a concise and effective of manner.

More troops were assembled and analysis conducted.

After grabbing their weapons and gear, the Sergeant and his men moved toward the hill through the Ardenne Forest. One man was at the point. All were watching and listening for any signs of danger. The enemy could be anywhere. Caution was essential but speed was a priority.

The enemy was relentless. The Germans searched the area for any resistance. They were regrouping on the eastern boundary for another assault. Heavy artillery was being transported to the lines for more precise bombardments.

All resistance needed to be eliminated.

Behind any tree or rock could be a threat. Every step was dangerous. Pressure was increasing and anxiety was becoming prominent. Nerves were on edge.

When dead Americans were encountered, ammunition and other supplies were removed from their bodies. Gunfire and explosions were heard as they again proceeded toward their objective through the fog. Any advantage was necessary for their survival.

For the dead, the war ended.

The front was collapsing but the Allies continued to fight, vigorously. Many were killed and others captured as the battle progressed. Resistance was brutal to the Germans. No one wanted glory. The common cause was not heroism. Their first predisposition was survival, which motivated them to continue.

Any person, who is thrown into a desperate situation, reacts on instinct. Training and procedures were important but immediate conflicts needed immediate responses. Too many unknowns of the conflict existed on the front. Any advantage was necessary to diminish the threat.

The patch of the 106th division signified their pride. It was the Golden Lions. It wasn't the emblem, which brought them honor. All divisions had different insignia and all fought with distinction during the conflict.

Blood and death showed no favorites.

One aspect of the patch was a foreshadowing of their cohesiveness. For those, who know, let them tell others. For the ones, who don't know, let understanding come. The gesture of the Lions elongated tongue told the story. If the enemy saw, they knew their fighting spirit in the face of adversity.

The patch signified their attitude and was their motto.

All divisions had courage and fortitude. All bleed and fought with their different patches, but the Golden Lions demonstrated their vigor and pride. The massive encounter with the enemy was unexpected. Even with the training, the odds were overwhelming. All concentrated on their specific objectives and performed with honor.

With the group photo at Camp Atterbury, expressions varied. Some smiled. Others were disgusted. A few were emotionless. Anguish was seen on others.   Enthusiasm was rare. None wanted war.

All were scared.

The realization of what was about to come was not within them.   These men never experienced the horrors of war, even if the possibilities were evident.

Can anyone, who lives within a peaceful existence, imagine a hell?

All realized the danger, but none knew anything, until they lived it.

The remaining men of squads one and two of the 2nd Platoon also retreated. They began to arrive at the hill to setup their defenses. More of the enemy was approaching. They were being surrounded. All was being prepared.

Ammunition wasn't plentiful but enough was available for their needs with the next encounter.

Iodine pills were used to decontaminate water sources, such as from rivers, lakes, and the snow.

Men were scattered. Disorganization was prevalent. Some soldiers ran for safety. Others retreated, before being needlessly killed. The command structure collapsed until many of the men banded together to help one another.

In a few areas all stood their ground until all were killed.

Two soldiers were running through the woods. They were trying to find a place of safety. Regrouping with others was a priority. Being alone was not an option. They were scared and lost.

Neither found a place to hide from the devastation.

They approached a small hill by a road.

Both were breathing heavily. A canvassed truck was traveling on the snow-covered road. It was approaching their position. As they were preparing to walk down the hill, sounds were heard of gunfire.

The truck driver lost control for a few moments as the truck veered toward the left and right. It continued down the road for a few more seconds, until it stopped.

Many Germans appeared and began to continue their assault.

"There's nothing; we can do," said one of the soldiers on the hill. "Not our fight."

"Poor buggers don't stood a chance," said the other man. "No sense being killed, needlessly."

"Let's get out of here."

They left the area and disappeared into the woods.

Another man was at a machine gun. German troops were advancing on his position. Within his mind, he had no chance to survive. They continued their advance.

He waited, aimed, and was ready to fire.

Time was his advantage.

There was nothing else; he could do, but kill them, before they overwhelmed his position. No other options existed. He continued to wait.

Pressure increased on the trigger.

If they wanted a fight, he'd give them one.

As they advanced, he waited, until they were in range, and then he began to fire. Bullets were sprayed toward them. He was relentless. The gun was continually waved back and forth toward the incoming troops. All his energy was channeled through the weapon. His facial expressions became more aggressive. He fired and fired as bullets flew past him.

More and more Germans began to fall. As bullets impacted their bodies, one after the other dropped to the ground. They were caught off guard. Even the ones, who were lying in the snow, were spayed with bullets. The element of surprise was the advantage. None had a chance, as he relentlessly continued his assault.

All the Germans appeared dead, but he continued to aggressively fire into the bodies.

Smoke billowed from the machine gun as he continued spray the area with bullets. Nothing stopped him until his safety was secure and all were positively dead. His death was certain, if the intensity was lacking. All his energy was channeled through the weapon. He became obsessed with his safety.

As he released the trigger, he eyes were affixed into the distance. His face showed no emotion. No movement was seen until he lowered his head.

When he was certain that the no one had any possibility of being alive, he was relieved and satisfied for his safety.

Sergeant Messmer and his men were continuing toward the hillside.

"You goof balls are lost, aren't you?" asked the Sergeant. "Too cold for a stroll with the Krauts behind us. Coburn, go that way!" The Sergeant yelled toward the point man. We're almost there. Didn't basic teach you knot heads anything?" he asked. He glanced in various directions, before saying, "The fog is in pockets. No one better use visibility, as an excuse."

The men continued to walk away from the front with many possible hazards. Their existence was for the moment. Each knew; the Germans were everywhere. Each watched their surroundings. Snipers or other hazards were a constant threat.

With any encounter with the enemy, all could be instantly killed.

Each man showed signs of distress from the battle and weather conditions but all were basically in pleasant moods. None knew the severity of the German assault. They concentrated on their survival. The initial attack was a disaster for the Germans. Hundreds of the enemy was killed with mortars, artillery, and weapons fire.

Even if the Americans were outnumbered, the enemy greatly suffered from the initial engagement.

As the tanks approached during the morning hours, they were in the trenches. The forest was behind them. The enemy approached from the fields. The advantage was with Americans. Even with the initial assault, most squads held their ground.

Many men were still pinned down across the entire sector.

Options were limited, except to wait until darkness. The leaders of their squad had an opportunity to destroy the threat. Their courage was a bold maneuver. Action needed to be taken, before all the men were killed. After discussing the possibilities, the risk was minimized. The possibility of death existed, but no other choices were available.

Sergeant Messmer and Staff Sergeant Waller thought the Germans were waiting for reinforcements. With the limited availability of ammunition and other supplies, everyone's survival was at risk. No other alternatives existed, except to eliminate the threat. A good chance existed for success, if the enemy was surprised. None would survive with another attack.

The temperature was below 20 degrees and snow was everywhere. Their footprints were imprinted with every step. Anyone could easily follow the markings. The risk was known but higher ground was a military advantage. As they proceeded toward their objective, happier times were remembered.

As Private Branson walked, he turned toward the man next to him, and softly said, "Dennis, when I was younger, I used to walk through the woods with my brother. We'd hunt rabbits. Good eating. My mom sure knew how to cook 'um."

"No one would dare walk anywhere with this weather," said Dennis Wooden. "Too cold even for rabbits."

"Do you think that we were daft?" asked Private Branson. "In the spring, when the grass was low. Those critters were much easier to spot. When cooked to perfection, the meat was so tender and juicy. Delicious."

"I had a pet rabbit, once," said Bob Bart, who walked behind them. "Disappeared one day. When I brought food, one morning, the cage door was open. Something smelled mighty fine from a house down the road, the next day. Never proved anything, but I never saw the rabbit again. Until my parents bought me a dog, I surely missed her. I was planning on selling the offspring, if I ever found her a proper mate. Picky, she was."

"Stop joshing, Bob," said Denise Wooden.

"True story," he said, as he smiled. "None truer."

"Sure," said Private Branson. "I could tell you about the time; my brother and I were on the lake. We were fishing for trout."

"Your family loves to eat," said Bob Bart, "If you're an example."

"You're right. A meal was an occasion. Anyway, as we fished, something was tugging on the line. Both of us tried to real it in. We thought, we had the biggest catch of our lives. It could have fed the family for weeks."

As Dennis Wooden smiled, he asked, "What kind of fish was it?"

"Never knew. The line broke. During one dry summer, the water regressed. A few old submerged tires were visible. Just a shattered reality."

As Dennis Wooden stared into the distance, he said, "Just like this. It's a beautiful scene with hidden hazards. What will be remembered? The beauty or the underlying reality?"

No other words were spoken.

While the men continued to walk, they observed their surroundings.

"Keep moving," said Sergeant Messmer. "Even with a compass, all of you would get lost."

"We're not lost," stated Corporal Smith. "Are we lost? No, the Sarge is fooling with us again."

Private Branson replied, "That tree looks familiar."

"All of you shut up!" the Sergeant loudly exclaimed. "We're almost there. Darkness will be worse than the fog." He smiled for a moment, before saying, "You want those Krauts to hear us. Just shut up! All of you keep your voices down. Your dirty hides will be your own responsibility. No appreciation. Just no appreciation for anything."

Only a few of the squad were killed during the first day. These were Cole Johnson, Ryan Lester, Donny Cole, and Staff Sergeant Bill Waller. Their deaths and others motivated them to continue their efforts. No one wanted to die. Regrouping on higher ground would be advantageous to prevent more deaths and face the enemy from a better vantage point.

The others in the squad were Sergeant John Messmer, Mel Stone, Corporal Jim Conroy, Ron Heady, Steven Rayburn, Bob Bert, Tom Larson, Corporal Jack Smith, Little Joe Banner, Private Kenneth Branson, Carl Jefferson, Ryan Smyth and Dennis Wooden.

The names have been forgotten, except for the families, who knew them. Time erased these men and their story from history, as other aspects of the war became more important. The individual dogfaces were not important to many historians, writers, and filmmakers. Their names and existence vanished from the record books, while the names of the major players in the war were brought to prominence.

Nothing is totally historically accurate.

The true events are in the minds of the ones, who lived to tell the story. Gaps exist and memories fade. Nothing can recreate reality. Only representations are presented with threads of truth. The individual has his own story, which is true from the person's perspective.

Facts must be compared and evaluated. History changes with the popularity of the moment. Reality only exists at any given time and then fades into oblivion. No one knows an individuals reality.

The squad finally arrived on the hill.

"Messmer!" shouted the Lieutenant. "Where have you been?"

"Taking a stroll with my men," he replied.

The Lieutenant aggressively asked, "What was the status in your area?"

"Full of dead Krauts and more on the way."

The Lieutenant glanced toward him and his men and then said, "You ready for more."

"Let 'um come. We'll old this hill," said the Sergeant, as the men stood behind him. "No one will deter us."

"Let your men rest for 10 minutes. Have a little grub before the next assault begins. Not much left, but you deserve it." After readjusting his gloves, he said, "Afterwards, dig in and then deploy your men along the ridgeline."

"Yes sir," the Sergeant stated, as the turned toward his men. "Take 10 and have some grub." He then asked the Lieutenant, "How's the ammo?"

"Not good. No reinforcements and supplies have arrived. Communications with the rear has been disrupted. The force of the enemy and the seriousness of their assault are not known." He glanced around their position,

66

before saying, "Not good, Sergeant. Not good at all."

"We can fight them off. We must hold this hill until reinforcements arrive."

"Messmer, you have guts. I'll access the situation, as the day progresses." The Lieutenant saluted, before saying, "Dismissed."

The Sergeant returned the gesture, and then said, "Yes sir." He began to walk toward his men.

"This lousy war," said Conroy, as he opened a can of processed meat. "Tastes like dog food. He turned toward the man next to him, who was eating the same thing, and then said, "How can you eat that stuff?"

Private Branson replied, "Delicious. Just be thankful for what we have. Nothing is worse."

"You make me sick," he said, as he began to eat from the container.

"Sarge, how are the rations?" asked Larson.

"We'll be fine, when supplies arrive."

"You mean, if they arrive," said Conroy.

The Sergeant sternly said, "We can take 'um. The situation is not hopeless. Do your job and stop worrying. We're holding."

Captain Grant was still within the pillbox. During the battle, his duty was to plan strategies and relay orders. No benefit would be gained with his death with unnecessary risks. The duty of his men was to kill the enemy, but his was to command.

The volatile situation was monitored from his command center. Reinforcements and supplies were desperately needed. Anxiety was increasing within him and his men. The enemy was regrouping for another attack.

The situation was dismal from the reports of recon patrols.

The men were scattered in various sectors. Most were spread out on the ridgeline for about a mile. One squad protected the pillbox. A few were still pinned down and unable to retreat. Others were regrouping.

The battle was very unpredictable. The enemy's strength was unknown. An advantage was needed. Nothing could be done. Waiting and praying were the only options.

The Captain's troops were weary and ready. The cohesion of the men was diminishing from the scars of battle and the losses. They needed hope and a leader with the courage to motivate them. A quick victory was needed. Without help, there was no hope. The squads would fight to the death, if necessary.

Positive enforcement was used to motivate them.

"Get on the line!" screamed the Lieutenant of Platoon 2. "To your positions! Be ready! You are the Golden Lions! Rip them to pieces!"

The sound of explosions and gunfire could be heard around them.

The Germans were continuing the attack and eliminating pockets of resistance throughout the region. No one was spared. Their objectives were to advance by defeating the allies and destroying their will to fight. If the lines were disrupted, no one could save their adversaries from surrender or death.

"We need help," said a soldier. "The Captain has it made. We could all be dead for all he cares."

"If the Captain was related to a movie actor," stated another soldier to his right, "maybe, he is protecting his complexion."

"I heard, someone ask him whether or not he was related to a famous actor," the first soldier replied. "The Captain was insulted and stated that no phony puny actor was related to him. He said that war is reality and not a dumb movie."

The second soldier amusingly said, "I never heard such truer words. He still should fight with us. He'd probably still get a medal and be promoted, either way."

Germans were approaching their position and all were ready to continue the battle. They were weary but the death of their friends escalated their determination. Many had confidence; they could hold their territory.

On the 16th of December, the remainder of three squads was on a hill overlooking the enemy. The Germans were approaching and the Americans opened fire. One by one, more Germans fell to the ground and were killed.

Sergeant Messmer used his Thompson and killed more Germans.

The men on both sides were relentless.

Ammunition was at dangerous levels, but the men continued to fire, until the enemy retreated. No unnecessary firing was tolerated. All the weapons were used, only if accuracy was assured. All knew that this was a temporary victory. Only a few rounds remained. Grenades were nonexistent. Hope was diminishing, if another assault occurred. The hill wasn't defendable without help.

Communications were non-existent with other divisions and companies. The condition of other sectors was still not known. If reinforcements and supplies could break through the lines, their victory would be assured.

No help was available, for now, and the enemy was surrounding their position.

"We will fight them to the last man!" shouted Sergeant Messmer toward his squad, as he chuckled. "Nazis filth!"

"Sarge, how can we continue?" asked Corporal Conroy.

"Our bear hands!" he replied, as explosions were heard in the distance. "We have to hold them until help arrives. All will be for nothing, otherwise."

Others had the same intense rage for their enemy. Adrenaline was high. Nerves were on the edge. Death was everywhere. Common sense was ignored for the greater cause of revenge and pride for the living and the dead. Reason was becoming suppressed. The battle was no longer about survival.

"If we die, who will know of us?" asked the Corporal.

The Sergeant stared toward each one of his men. All had different expressions. They were dirty and worn with a weakened spirit. Courage was still seen beneath their outward demeanor. Hopelessness was seen from their eyes.

A piece treaty was Hitler's motive with the offensive with an expanded Germany territory. The Axis surprised the Allies. His troops were pushing west but pockets of resistance remained. The courage of the few, who held their ground, caused reinforcements to eventually arrive, but not immediately. The 80,000 men, who were initial involved in the battle, grew to over 600,000 by the end of January 1945.

Bastogne was a recognized example of courage, pride, and determination by the American forces. They withstood constant bombardment. Tanks surrounded their position but they wouldn't surrender.

American troops were pushed back to the Meuse River. Soldiers continued the fight who were scattered across the western front. Their bravery diverted the attention of the invaders. Most wanted to stand their ground and destroy the enemy. Without food, supplies, and ammunition, the fight ended for many with surrender or death.

As the Germans advanced, the resistance needed to end. More troops and equipment were needed in other areas. Losses were heavy and a swift solution was needed to end the threat. The solution was an ultimatum from the Germans to the resistors to surrender or die.

Other concerns were a hazard to the allies. The night before the battle, German paratroopers were dropped behind enemy lines. These were not ordinary Germans. They knew fluent English and were dressed, as Americans. After infiltrating western sectors, they created confusion.

Word spread quickly of the ploy, but to those, who were unaware disaster occurred, when the unsuspecting were killed.

Signs were changed and misdirection given to the Americans by the infiltrators.

A few disguised Germans drove threw the lines without incident.

The remaining members of the three squads were prepared for the next advance, before the pitch black of the night came. With a limited supply of food and ammo, the attack would be disastrous. All would be killed. There was no hope unless help arrived.

The minutes seemed like an eternity.

"What are they waiting for?" asked Sergeant Messmer, as he turned toward one of his men. "You have a family, Smith?"

"A wife and three wonderful children."

"What's your profession?"

"Store owner," Smith replied. "Keeps me busy. I have a great wife. Beautiful one."

He retrieved a photo from under his coat and showed the Sergeant.

"Nice," he said, "I wish; the right woman will come for me."

"No steady."

"Not really," said the Sergeant. "Just playing the field. Women are attracted to me, like bees to honey. The right one is waiting for me, somewhere. We'll both need each other. Someday, we'll meet at the right moment." He paused, before saying, "You're in your forties, aren't you?"

"Was 48, this year," said Smith. "I was drafted, like all the rest. Didn't think that I'd be here, though. I thought that I'd stay in the states."

"No guarantees for anyone."

"Suppose not."

"There's too much death," said the Sergeant. "There must be something more."

"Life or death, Sarge. This is our Alamo. What else is there?"

"An inner peace with a loving family. Hell has no peace. Echoes of this madness are within me. Will we ever forget? I have never seen so much misery." The Sergeant glanced down the hill, "Just body parts and blood. At one moment, we're alive and the next moment, we're dead. Our existence is so fragile. Who can save us?"

"You believe in God?" asked Smith.

The Sergeant replied, "Yes, I'm Catholic. Not too obedient, but I believe. Everything is so hollow. Is there more to know?"

"Don't know. I just thought, if you accept him, you're saved, as long as you do, as he does."

"What's God's plan for us?" asked the Sergeant. "Too many have died. We have to continue the fight. I pray for help but there's no hope. The reinforcements must come. Doesn't God care?"

"I suppose; the Krauts are praying for victory."

The Sergeant stared down the hill, observed the dead Germans, and then smiled, before saying, "Didn't do them any good."

"Maybe, the question should be, what's God plan for each one of us," stated Rayburn. "God has his own battle plan and knows what everyone needs. All is revealed in time."

"We have no time," Sergeant Messmer disgustingly said. "Those Krauts are brutal. We must fight the enemy to the end. We must succeed for our men. They have killed too many of us, already. A few more won't make any difference. Why doesn't God listen? Lord, let your will be done. If it's your will; we die, let us die."

"They're probably giving us time to make peace with God," said Private Branson. "They may be deliberately taunting us. Just waiting to pick our bones. We'll know soon enough. Without rations, no meat will be left. Maybe, we'll all die of starvation, if they wait too long."

Smith replied, "You eat more than all of us. He turned toward him, before saying, "Nice hearty meal."

"Watch it!" yelled Branson. "Use one of the Krauts. You guys are loonies."

All of them laughed.

"I saw something in those trees," said the Sergeant.

"Where?" Smith asked.

The Sergeant pointed in the distance.

"Be ready for another attack," Private Branson stated.

"Just keep your eyes open," said the Sergeant.

Smith stated, "Mine are frozen. My whole body is chilled. Hands numb." He grabbed snow, and then said, "My kids would love this. Perfect for them. We had a few good snowball fights. One time, they built one of the biggest snowman."

The Sergeant turned toward him. "From the other side of the glass, the snow is beautiful," he said.

After a few moments of silence, Rayburn stated, "They know; we're cut off. Every skirmish wastes ammunition. Who knows how many men are at their disposal?"

Wooden nervously said, "We're all dead,"

Explosions and weapons fire were heard all around their location.

Platoon 2 was on a hill to the west of the German advance.

Until darkness approached, the enemy continued their assault.

Most of Company F retreated to a ridge of hills. These forces were spread out and many were cutoff. The topographical geography in this region was irregular. This area was highly defendable in many locations. Some of the troops had enough ammunition, food, and other supplies to continue to hold the Germans for days.

The concentration of troops within the region of the Elsenborn Ridge to the north contained the 2nd infantry and 99th infantry.

All along the 80-mile front, the Americans pounded the German advance, until more surrendered or were killed. The strong will and resistance of the Allies wasn't anticipated by the Germans. The advance was delayed and the reduction of equipment, men, and ammunition on both sides affected the outcome.

The temperatures may have affected the functionality of some weapons. Moisture may have caused malfunctions. Problems occurred for the Allies and Germans. No one was spared from inconveniences in the abnormal conditions.

The fog covered the valley and forest toward the east. The bottom portions of the trees were engulfed with mist. The upper sections were exposed and the sky was overcast.

Everything seemed surreal.

Visibility was worse in the lower regions.

The men waited and many felt the same, as Sergeant Messmer.

They wanted to defend their position, even if they were killed. None knew the force of the Germans. The odds were staggering. The scope of the invasion was massive. The enemy needed to be stopped.

The transformation was worthy to note. Their first sensations were to survive. After casualties increased, pride became prominent. Freedom had no influence on the attitude of the men, who wanted to continue the fight. None were fighting for freedom and capitalism. Their focus became revenge for their fallen brothers.

The Germans were dealing with other areas of resistance. Some areas had more priority. The delay was hurting their advance. The strong will of the American forces was damaging to their strategies. The pockets of resistance needed to be eliminated.

Only two choices were offered from the Germans to the Allies.

Chapter Four: The Surrender

Periods of less intensity did occur with no major incidents. Both sides needed the time to regroup. Strategies needed to be changed. These moments were only temporary.

The unexpected gave no one peace.

As the day began to end, the men continued to defend their position. The Germans continued the assault. The forces engaged at random intervals. Tensions were increasing. Darkness was approaching. The men were prepared to continue the fight, as the first day ceased.

Holding their position was desirable, until help arrived, but only a few rounds remained, which was only used with extreme accuracy.

Many of the men from Company F retreated during the nighttime hours of the first day. The areas, which were not defendable, were evacuated earlier. The Germans broke through the lines at various locations and were a constant threat. The men could easily be surrounded and trapped. Spontaneous decisions needed to be contemplated by the men and the officers.

Ammunition was dangerously low.

The light, which illuminated their adversary, would soon be gone.

One soldier noticed with his binoculars, a German soldier, walk from the woods into the clearing. He then shouted, "Lieutenant, over there!" He pointed into the distance toward the man.

A German officer was slowly walking into the clearing, while waving a white flag.

"Maybe, they're surrendering," shouted Private Branson.

"Fat chance," said Sergeant Messmer.

Smyth stated, "One easy target." He pointed his rifle toward the German.

"No firing," stated the Sergeant. "Let's find out what they want."

The Lieutenant attached a white handkerchief to a broken tree branch and then walked down the hill. He proceeded cautiously as both approached each other in the fog. The stood in the clearing and talked for a few moments. The men observed no expressions of hostility.

"Boy, we've had it," Corporal Conroy stated. "Not good at all. What do you think, Sarge?"

"We'll find soon enough," he replied.

"The Lieutenant should negotiate for food," Private Branson said.

"You have enough blubber to live longer than all of us," stated Little Joe, as he adjusted his helmet. He opened his canteen and drank a few gulps, before saying, "Hardly no water left."

Corporal Conroy grabbed some snow and threw it at the other soldier, before saying, "We have plenty."

"Just shut up," said Little Joe. "Wise guy."

The Lieutenant began to walk away from the encounter as the German officer proceeded toward his men. The Americans saw disgust on his face. The mannerisms of his movements weren't encouraging. Hopelessness was apparent.

All knew; the alternatives weren't encouraging.

After returning, he called all the noncommissioned officers in a meeting. All approached him and waited for him to speak. They wanted to know the results of the meeting. Anxiety overwhelmed their emotions.

"The Kraut told me," said the Lieutenant, "we have until morning to surrender or be killed by artillery. I asked for other concessions. No other terms were offered, except that the critically wounded would be given medical care. He told me that the walking wounded must leave the hill."

"Damn them to hell," said Master Staff Sergeant Clifton.

Sergeant Messmer stated, "We'll fight with our bear hands and use our bayonets."

"Don't be a fool!" shouted the Lieutenant.

"Jackass!" the Sergeant shouted. "We can take 'um!"

"Watch your mouth, Messmer," the Lieutenant stated. "Under other circumstances, I'd take your stripes."

"We can take 'um," the Sergeant softly repeated.

"We'll die, needlessly," Sergeant Watson said. "Nothing will remain."

"Can we evacuate?" asked Master Staff Sergeant Clifton.

"No," stated the Lieutenant, "the Krauts have us cutoff in sections along the ridge. Their officer told me that we're totally isolated and surrounded. The rest will suffer a similar fate."

"Surrender is our only option," Staff Sergeant Watson stated.

Others offered their input, before the Lieutenant said, "We have no chance. The men have had it." He briefly looked toward each one, smiled, and then said, "I'm proud of you and your men for your courage and determination. I have the responsibility. We're cut off from the Captain. His last communication was to hold our position until no other options existed. No choice remains. Military protocol must be followed. I'll inform the Kraut in the morning; we accept surrender. Destroy all weapons and bury what little ammo remains. Inform your men. A truce exists until 9AM. Dismissed."

"I'd love to bury more rounds in their hides," mumbled Sergeant Watson, as he walked from the others.

Sergeant Messmer walked toward a tree and angrily slammed his rifle and then his Thompson against a tree trunk, until both weapons broke into fragments. The debris fell into the snow. After staring toward the broken pieces for a few moments, he proceeded toward his men to relay the order.

After considering the options, all thought; the correct alternative was made. Some of the men still wanted to stay and fight. Tempers were still raging. All accepted their fate. If they had a chance to survive, the decision would have been interpreted differently. Needlessly dying wasn't an enjoyable option.

No other choice existed.

The strategy was the same in other areas across the 80-mile front.

Any Americans, who refused to surrender, were killed. No mercy was shown, if the men continued the fight. Whether the Germans were showing some mercy or just saving ammunition, was not known. With the correct coordinates, all the soldiers would have been killed in a short time.

No other choices needed to be given.

Between death and survival, the correct alternative was life. The battle was over for Platoon Two. The men fought bravely. Although, they lost the battle, the war continued.

There was no shame in their decision.

Disappointment engulfed many of the men. The battle ceased for them. Nothing could be done. The men of different backgrounds and beliefs fought for survival. Emotions were transformed into pride and revenge for the humiliation. All were surprised by the attack. The response of the men was courageous and honorable.

"We're better off," said Stone. "No more will die."

"Those Krauts aren't trustworthy," Corporal Conroy stated, as he raised himself from his foxhole and then leaned his back against a tree. "Should we die, like cattle or men?"

Stone replied, "A quick and honorable death is better than a prolonged misery, before an undignified death."

A few others of the squad walked toward him.

"They must be bluffing," said Private Branson. "We devastated them. Bodies are splattered across the forest. Maybe, only a few Krauts remain. If he was the lone survivor, he'd probably receive a medal for his deceit."

Sergeant Messmer walked toward the group, and then said, "The Lieutenant's decision stands, whether we like it or not." He paused, and then continued his words, "We really showed 'um. I am proud of all of you. The war is over for us. We had our turn. Let others continue the fight."

"Too many of our boys lost it," said Stone. "All good men. Donny Cole was just married. His gal was gorgeous. He never had time for a honeymoon. He was 20 years old and still pure. Now, he will never experience any affection. A good woman gives much pleasure."

"Ryan Lester was just a wet nosed kid," said Corporal Smith. "Just snuffed out."

The Sergeant said, "His torment ended."

"Amen," said Corporal Smith.

"There are too many for us to handle," Rayburn stated, "One artillery round could finish us."

"The dead have no misery and shame," Corporal Smith stated.

Corporal Conroy, as he lit a cigarette, stated, "They were the lucky ones."

"We'll be fine," stated Sergeant Messmer. "Just relax and have one more night of freedom. Individuals soldiers, like us, will win the war. More will keep coming and dying. The march toward Berlin will continue. The enemy will be defeated. Liberation will come."

"I don't know about any of you poor slobs," said Private Branson, "Dry clothes and some good chow are better than what we have now. My bones are chilled." He kicked his foot in the snow. "My feet are numb." He momentarily groaned, before continuing, "I had some German sausage and potato salad in the States. Very delicious."

"We should be so lucky," Corporal Conroy stated.

"Not possible?" asked Private Branson.

Rayburn slapped his helmet and then replied, "Very doubtful."

"Hey, Sarge," said Private Branson, "what do you think?"

"We'll know soon enough," he said, as he smiled.

"I can smell it now," said the Private. "Medium rare steaks with my Dad's special sauce. He barbecued every few weeks in the summer. I smelled the aroma, while I walked home from school. Delightful. Melted in your mouth."

"What made it special?" asked Corporal Smith.

"He'd use cheap beer," the Private replied. "Garlic was coated on the meat. He knew someone at the market for a special rate on various cuts. Always the best from my dad."

Everyone laughed.

Darkness overwhelmed them.

The sun was never seen, but the light was evident, until the brightness decreased. Darkness overwhelmed them. The night came quickly and the day seemed a faint memory. Nothing was seen in the distance. The area was pitch black. Even if the moon gave light, it couldn't penetrate the overcast skies.

Flashlights and lanterns were used to illuminate the area.

"I want all the weapons broken by morning," Sergeant Messmer stated. "Bury any extra rounds and anything else; the enemy can use."

"In this frozen ground," said Private Branson. "I had enough trouble with the foxhole."

"Just do it!" shouted the Sergeant. "Use your shovels and bayonets! He glanced toward all of them, and then said, "Save what little rations remain. What's ahead of us is unknown." He walked away, and then softly stated, "Good men," before smiling.

"Not enough rations to feed anyone," said Smith. "With no food or ammunition, I'd rather surrender."

The 106th had a 27-mile front to defend. Many troops defended St. Vith. They courageously defended the town during the bombardment and the advancing enemy. The allies were given a chance to regroup from their gallant efforts.

Many died with their bravery.

Many towns were under siege, but all the units fought with courage. They postponed the advance and depleted the enemy of their resources. As the Germans proceeded, they had no choice to destroy any resistance. As buildings crumbled, the defenders continued their fight. They had more supplies to hold the enemy.

Artillery and tanks shelled the towns.

No hope existed for the forces unless help arrived. They continued their vigil with the hope of supplies and other necessities being parachuted to their locations. With the weather, planes were grounded. Many prayed for their needs, as they continued the fight.

The men of the division were on the line for many days. They arrived on December 10th in the town of St Vith, before being deployed to the line, which was the crowned ridge of the Schnee Eifel. This was in a forested area in the Ardennes.

The distance from the city was about 12 miles.

These men had never experienced combat. Only minor altercations occurred, before the offensive. None of the men thought that they would be under such hardship. The area was quite for about 2 months. Most thought, they would have an easy time with the deployment to guard the boundary.

None expected such a massive assault.

Since D-Day, the Germans were being pushed back to their homeland and many Americans thought the Germans lost their will to fight.

Sergeant Messmer looked toward his dog tags. The serial number was 37392427. It was required to be memorized. Name, rank, and serial number were the only information to be given to the enemy. Nothing else must be stated. All other information was suppressed from his memories. Anything could be used against the Allies to further the cause of the Third Reich.

In an unconventional way, he obeyed orders. His duties were always taken seriously. He never wavered from his responsibilities. His safety was a concern. A priority was wisdom and carefulness with his surroundings. He was always a happy person with a good sense of humor and loyal to his duties.

He always cared about others and the men in his squad. If he had no choice, he did what he had to do. No stealing was permitted from anyone. His moral code was engrained into his inner being from his parents and by experience.

His Dad emigrated from Germany and his Mom was of Dutch decent. Both were strict as all parents were in those days. They were raised in a different era when obedience was important. No impropriety was tolerated in public, such as swearing and drinking. Ridicule occurred, if women and children were exposed to inappropriate behavior.

Everything had a time and place.

The war was changing his perspective. The horror affected him. He needed an inner peace and stability. This nightmare never could be imagined. A person lives and a person dies. He needed more to fill the hollowness, which brought everyone to death.

As the Sergeant sat by a tree, he remembered a song, which was heard on the radio. He began to softly sing the lyrics. A few in his squad, who were resting, heard him and began to sing. A few just hummed the melody, while others sang the lyrics. More heard and joined the chorus. The other squads followed the example and most sang, as one voice, which echoed from the ridge.

Many men were remembering their experiences in their hometowns, Camp Atterbury, Indiana, and the trip to England on the Queen Mary.

When they arrived in England on November 17th, 1944, a train was boarded. They traveled past beautiful white cliffs, which brought them to Adelstrop. They lived in Quanset huts until the men were assigned to the front.

All of the 106th landed in France on December 6, 1944 and then replaced the 2nd infantry division on the line on the 11th. Only 5 days separated the division and others from their destiny. Most were well-trained green recruits. Nothing prepared them for what was about to happen. None wanted to be killed and all were scared at various degrees.

When the fighting began, these managers, farmers, sales people, clerks, accountants, storeowners, and others, became soldiers. Most performed with distinction even in the chaotic conditions. As they were attacked, they were forced to fight. Much courage was exhibited with the risk of death to save themselves or others. Many were killed and others shed their blood to stand their ground and stop the Nazis threat.

Before leaving, the 106th, the men received 8-months of training at Camp Atterbury, which was by the town of Edinburgh. They were ready and weary from their experiences. None knew what awaited them. Many were eager to perform their duties.

The possibility of death haunted them but all thought the German threat was contained. The men did not know the experiences of war, except from books, newsreels, the movies, and military propaganda. They didn't have first hand knowledge of the horror. If they did, maybe more hesitation would have affected their behavior in battle. Without prior knowledge of battle conditions, they performed with honor and pride.

Italian and German prisoners were interred at the facility in the States. A barb wired compound to the west of the main training camp enclosed them. The ones, who died, were buried on the grounds. The food varied depending on their customs. All were treated with respect and dignity. Troublemakers were handled, properly, by placing them in isolation.

After arriving in England, many company hikes were taken for exercise. On occasion, the town was visited. Trucks, which were 1 /12 tons, were used to transport the men. The training was brief from November to December of 1944, but their skills needed to be sharpened and enhanced.

The main force of the attack was directed toward the 106th and within a month of fighting about 8.663 men was killed in various areas.

Sergeant Messmer was drafted and then inducted in October of 1942. During his service, he was transferred to various camps, which were Camp Carson in Salina, Kansas, Fort Custer in Michigan, Fort Ord in California, and then finally

Camp Atterbury in Indiana. As an MP, he guarded prisoners and performed other duties. Enforcing military law was a priority and keeping the peace. After arriving in England, he was promoted to Sergeant with the squad number of #653.

About 2 years of experience in the military was gained, before the offensive.

A medic helped the wounded. All of them needed more care. Some injuries were worse than others. Only basic first aid was provided. Nothing else could be done, until they were transferred to Aid stations.

One of the wounded painfully asked, "Can we trust them?"

"We have no choice," replied the medic, as he changed his bandage. "Bleeding has stopped." After applying the tape, an expression of hopelessness appeared, before he said, "You need professional help. If we all die, noting will be gained."

"Doc, don't like being treated by them."

"I suppose, Doctors are the same everywhere," he said. "If we can trust them, I don't know. You'll be dead, soon, if those wounds aren't properly treated."

"I just don't like spending the rest of the war in a P.O.W. camp."

"Me, neither."

"If it just wasn't so cold," said the wounded man. "I'm chilled to the bone."

The medic closed the man's coat, before saying, "Our fight is finished. Just rest. By tomorrow, you'll be in a warm bed."

The wounded man smiled, as the medic walked from him.

As the medic approached the Lieutenant, he said, "Some of the men won't survive the night."

"Do the best; you can for them."

"Most want to walk with us, as we surrender," said the medic.

"That's fine. Let them walk with pride."

"We need stretchers for the others. Not advisable to carry them."

"The Kraut told me to leave the seriously wounded," said the Lieutenant. "Our medics will have to attend to the needs of the others."

"Can we trust them?"

"No alternatives."

"Better the fighting is over," said the medic. "Just too much brutality. All will be scarred for life."

"All will have to accept it. The memories will never escape any of us."

"Those are frightening thoughts," the medic sadly stated.

The weather and their defeat to the enemy caused most of the men to be restless. Many just stayed within their foxholes and others found warmth with their comrades by huddling together. They tried to stay as warm, as possible. The possibilities of what awaited them caused negative emotions.

Some remembered the Thanksgiving dinner at the British Camp in England, which was a disaster. The food appeared wonderful. All were appreciative for the meal. As they consumed the food, stomachs became upset. Everyone developed diarrhea and had to run to the facilities. Others used the rail on the outside of the mess hall to relieve themselves.

One soldier tried to describe the situation to his wife, but the letter was censored and all that remained was a troop movement.

The spoiled potatoes were probably the cause.

All finally realized, spending the rest of the war, as a P.O.W., was better than dying for nothing.

Various units of the 106th Division were in pockets across the region. Individuals tried to regroup. The ones on the line, who survived, retreated to higher ground and were given the same choices. Some chose the second option of death.

The Americans were scattered on various hills and in St. Vith, which was under siege, as Bastogne and other cities.

One group of 500 soldiers from the 106th was eventually forced to surrender by the Germans on December 20. Some men of Company F were included. They resided on a hill, before they were detected. Since the strength of the enemy forces were overwhelming, the only options were to surrender or die.

A few soldiers were sent on recon patrols to access and report about the scope of the offensive throughout the battlefield.

Most didn't know the severity of the invasion. Most thought that the battle was concentrated within their defensive positions. Very few realized, Hitler invaded from Southern Belgium to Luxembourg.

The Germans humiliated the Allies with the surprise attack. The courage and determination of the defenders with the endless supply of men and equipment was a determining factor to eventually win the battle at the end of January.

Before morning on the next day, the men of Platoon 2 broke all their weapons against the trees. No advantages were given to the Germans. The remaining ammunition and other useful items were buried. All units, which surrendered, were required by military regulations to perform the same procedure.

Some men helped each other to dispose of the supplies.

"Go deeper," said Sergeant Messmer to one of his men. "Keep going."

"My grave should be so deep," said Private Branson.

The Sergeant smiled, before saying, "The fallen aren't that fortunate."

The sound of weapons hitting the trees was heard. One man grabbed a rifle, and then passed it to another man, who slammed it against a tree. Others laid items in a pile for others to bury. All were helping each other by performing different tasks.

Prayers were said over the dead.

About one hour after sunrise, the Lieutenant met the German officer in the clearing. He informed him that his men would surrender. The officer told him that his men should march single file from the hill with their hands on their helmets. No weapons were allowed and the Lieutenant was assured; all the wounded, who couldn't walk, would receive medical care.

Many of the men watched from the ridge, as the Lieutenant continued the conversation.

All the men were ready to surrender but were hesitant. No one trusted the enemy. No other options existed. Prayers were prevalent from the ones, who needed comfort.

Some of the wounded were able to stand, while the worst cases remained. Many insisted on walking without help. Some of them needed to be supported. Before asking for asistance, a few stumbled. All expressions showed disgust but pride for their accomplishments overwhelmed their emotions.

Many limped and others bled, as they prepared to end their ordeal, but the end was just the beginning. The men didn't know what awaited them. The future was concealed and the motives of the Germans unclear. All could have been killed, but luckily or divinely, this group of Germans was not cold-blooded killers.

The enemy seemed to show mercy and compassion by giving them a choice. No one at the time knew the Germans motives. All were suspicious and scared. Their choices were limited. All alternatives could have resulted in their deaths. Even if all were killed, the best choice was to surrender.

The Allies killed many Germans during the battle. Ammunition was being depleted on both sides. Too many men were killed. All resources of the Germans were needed for proper military objectives. As the Americans held their positions, equipment and men were diverted to these troublesome areas. Valuable time was wasted. These obstacles were a burden on the Third Reich and their plans for conquest.

If they deployed more artillery to eliminate the pockets of resistance, more time was wasted.   German Soldiers were needed, who could be the next victims.   Too many died for their offensive. The advance was being delayed. All advantages were necessary for victory.

The Americans were given an opportunity to surrender to save resources for more important objectives.   Individual Germans commanders accessed each situation, differently.   Reactions may have been less merciful with resistors in other vital areas.

The Lieutenant was assured all his men would he treated within the rules of the Geneva Convention.

The men began to walk from the hill in single file with their hands on their heads. All were a few steps behind the other. They walked slowly, as the Germans advanced toward them. After a few minutes, the survivors of Platoon 2 were standing in the clearing and being searched.

The German officer told the Lieutenant; his decision was the proper one. Others, who defied common sense, were immediately killed from the artillery. None had a chance unless they surrendered. For them, the war ceased for the moment. As the Germans continued their assault and proceeded to victory, all would be safe in Germany.

"Those Krauts," Private Branson whispered, "have a certain stink."

Corporal Conroy softly replied, "We'll have to adjust."

"Shut up, you knuckleheads," Sergeant Messmer quietly said. "Don't provoke them."

The Germans scrutinized their prisoners very carefully. Each was asked to remove their coat and boots within extreme weather conditions. Helmets were removed and thrown to the ground. All were carefully frisked, as other soldiers pointed rifles toward them. The men were reluctant but cooperative. As the inspections continued, there were no options. They had to comply or die.

Captain Grant was on a different hill.

He refused to leave his bunker, until choices were limited, and then he stayed within a foxhole with others. Some say that he was ordered to return to the larger part of the company, before his area was surrounded. Only 9 officers and 70 men were at his disposal with no chance of a proper defense. The rest of the company either surrendered or were killed.

After many other areas were neutralized, the Germans eventually picked up his small group, a few days later.

He felt that the rest of the company abandoned him. All were scattered in various locations. The command structure was shattered. In the confusion, all the squads and men did what they had to do in order to survive.

Other pockets of resistance didn't surrender and fought to the last man. The opposition killed the defenders with artillery or troops. Their decision brought death. With the emotions from the battle, many, like Sergeant Messmer, refused to accept the inevitable.

Many wanted to continue to fight. Reasoning and common sense prevailed, which saved lives. These men eventually realized surrender was the only option. No one wanted to die for nothing.

Prisoners were captured and killed throughout the area. The elite SS troops were responsible for a well-known execution on the 17th of December. The Eastern front was more affected by these incidents. No one knew the reasoning for the massacre.

Other killings of unarmored prisoners did occur. Most of these incidents were not well known. The bodies were recovered at Malmedy in the middle of January 1945. The scene of the frozen corpses in the snow was a horrifying scene.

Death and mutilation were common in many areas. This incident was not comparable to anything else. The men had no weapons and were no threat. They were deliberately killed for no purpose. The incident enraged all, who witnessed and survived the event, and others, who were told the story.

The men were unarmed and taken to a field. Most were unaware, until machine guns became visible in the back of trucks. All were stunned for a moment, before trying to run in the snow. Rounds were fired toward them. By some estimates, 80 were killed, while others escaped into the woods.

One man eventually crossed a road and then ran toward a farmhouse. A German soldier spotted him, who stood on the road by the fence. A pistol was drawn and aimed toward the American.

It failed to fire.

The American eluded capture. He ran into the distance. No one pursued him.

The horror continued with the ones who were wounded. They lay in the snow with the dead bodies of other soldiers. A few cried for help and others moaned in anguish and desperation. As German trucks passed the field, the troops saw the movement of the wounded. As the cries for help continued, rounds were fired toward them without mercy.

None needed help anymore.

A few rumors did eventually flourish within the Allied forces.

These deliberate acts of violence were difficult to comprehend. In the heat of battle, anything could happen. When the situation was controlled and the threat removed, purposely killing someone was unthinkable. Within the thoughts of most soldiers, only madmen could commit such acts of violence. In the heat of battle, anything could happen on both sides.

In the early stages of the offensive, no one knew some prisoners were targeted for death, which may have affected their decision to surrender. If they were going to die, either way, then the only alternative was to fight with honor, even if death occurred.

The prisoners from different sectors were marched to Pruen, Germany at various intervals and slept in one of the buildings. The next day, they were marched 15 miles to Geroelstein and stayed in a barn on the perimeter of the town.

Chapter Five: The Barn

As the American lines collapsed, men from various sectors were marched to Geroelstein, a major railroad hub. Some men were taken to other cities. The time of the march varied, which depended on their location. A few days were required for the journey for the men from Company F and the others, who merged with them.

The men walked in different groups at different times.

Many were captured from various locations on the front. The American medics helped the less seriously wounded. Before proceeding to the destination, some rested within buildings or outside in the elements.

The weather was freezing and the roads snow covered.

Not everyone was captured from the various divisions. Some squads were able to leave their positions. Many were killed, if they didn't surrender. Even with minimal supplies, a few units attempted to find the American lines under fluidic conditions. With the advancing German forces, the task was difficult, but not impossible with the ingenuity of individual men and their courage.

A Private and an officer with 20 other men from the 423rd were separated from their unit. After fierce encounters with the German troops, they needed to retreat through enemy held territory on the 18th of December. The enemy was all around their position. No help existed.

The chances of survival were slim.

The fighting, since the invasion, depleted their food and ammunition. All needed to defend themselves against the enemy. Without proper nourishment, their strength was declining. Retreating was the only possibility for survival. As they proceeded toward their objective, dangers awaited them.

With the weather conditions, more adequate clothing was needed.

As the men advanced toward the lines, a Private for two days and nights scouted for the enemy. If the Germans were seen, he'd return and inform them of their position. Without a proper defense, the enemy needed to be avoided. Combat wasn't an option with their limited capabilities.

"Krauts are about a mile toward the east," he told the officer. He pointed toward another area, and then said, "Our best possibility for now. The terrain is more rugged. We'll bypass their encampment."

"Keep us informed," the officer stated. "If we're discovered, we'll have no chance."

The Private started to walk toward through the trees to continue his mission.

As the hours passed, he carefully checked the terrain. The men continued their retreat under his guidance. The enemy never noticed their movements through the occupied territories. Everyone was anxious to arrive safely. As they approached their lines, hopes were increasing for success.

After safely reaching American territory, sounds of gunfire were heard. Germans and armored units were attacking from the rear. At the last moment, their worst fears were realized. With the possibility of death, a defensive measure was initiated. After the officer left to report the attack, the Private reorganized the men to divert their fire and hold the position.

Reinforcements were desperately needed to defeat the Germans.

While the men waited for help, the battle raged. The courage, which was demonstrated, prevented the enemy from advancing. Since they had no other encounters, enough ammunition was available to hold their position. The fight continued and the Private was wounded. As reinforcements arrived, the Germans were defeated.

The wounded were taken to medical facilities and the Private honored for his courageous actions.

Over 23.000 were captured or missing from the conflict. As the men walked, they felt relieved and safe from the offensive. All were taken to an available holding area.

They were waiting to be transported to Bad Orb by Prison Camp IX-B. This camp was the main processing facility. Many others were transported to other locations, which depended on the availability of space.

The massive influx of men wasn't anticipated. The prison camps were becoming overcrowded. Different nationalities, such as the Russians, British, and Americans, were detained at these facilities.

Although relieved, the men in the barn felt humiliated.

In their minds, no more bullets, shrapnel, and/or explosions would harm them. They were safe from the violence. Most felt defeated and not useful to the outcome. None still realized the massiveness and purpose of the attack.

The enemy forces were too overwhelming in their sectors to continue the fight.

Although they were surprised by the attack, they fought with vigor. Surrender was their only choice. Many wanted to continue the confrontation. If they continued, none would have any worries. All would have been killed with artillery. The enemy forces were too strong for success, especially with no food or ammunition to sustain their defensive posture.

Conflicts were within their thoughts.

When they arrived outside the city, the men's names, rank, and serial numbers were recorded. The German shoulders took all their possessions including money, personal items, and a limited amount of rations. Confiscations were common with all the men. The Germans took what they needed and discarded other items. The Americans became agitated with their behavior.

They sat on the floor in the barn and waited for their transportation and assignment to a prison camp. All were individuals. The command structure of the units ceased to exist. They were now under the authority of their captors.

Telegrams were eventually sent to the relatives in the States. The men, who were captured, were initially stated, as missing in action. As more information became available, the status was changed to prisoner of war. Parents and wives were hopeful with the first telegram. The second brought relief from the possibility of the death of their loved one.

Military personnel in the States were assigned to visit the next of kin for the men, who were killed in action, if definite proof was available. This was not an easy assignment. The news was unbearable to the relatives. All had their duty and knew that death was unavoidable.

The relatives needed to be personally informed and comforted.

The parents of Sergeant Messmer were no exception. A telegram was received on January 12, 1945, which stated, "The secretary of war desires me to express his deep regret that your son, Sergeant John A. Messmer has been reported missing in action since sixteen December in Germany. If further details or other information are received, you will be promptly notified from Dunlop, the Adjutant General."

On March 27, 1945 another telegram was received, which stated, "Based on information received through the Provost Marshal, the general records of the war department have been amended to show your son, Sergeant John A. Messmer, a prisoner of war of the German Government. Any further information received will be furnished by the Provost Marshal, General J. A. Blio, the Adjutant General."

Time elapsed from the initial capture, which caused the relatives to have anguish, unless letters were received from their loved ones. The situation was volatile, plus the Germans needed to relay the information to the proper authorities. Everyone used newsreels, radio, and/or short wave communication for current information about the war.

The task was not easy to identify bodies and organize the records.

Dog tags were sometimes removed by the commanding officer. If those men were captured or killed the process was more difficult. Some of the ID's were blown away from the bodies from the blasts and still fastened, as they were buried in the snow. A few were melted beyond recognition from intense heat. Other tags were not found for other reasons.

Photographs and personal items were important identification tools.

Carnage and destruction were everywhere. Some men still lay where they fell. Others were shredded. A few were charred beyond recognition. Only pieces remained of some of the men.

The task was gruesome.

Identification was necessary for the military and families.

Sergeant Messmer sat with a few others in the corner of the barn.

Like cattle, they were being contained, until they were allowed to board the boxcars, which would transport them to Bad Orb. The ordeal was horrific. Bread and watery soup was the only food. None had access to shower facilities or toilets. The clothes were dirty and worn.

No heat was in the barn.

At least, they were alive and within a shelter, which was more pleasurable, than dying for nothing.

As more men from Company F and other soldiers were captured across the front, the influx of prisoners was increasing. Other barns and warehouses in the area were used for the ones, who surrendered. The P.O.W.'S were taken to different cities to board the trains, which depended on the location of their capture.

As time progressed, misery increased. The men were becoming restless as facilities were being prepared for the prisoners. The Germans were not prepared for the overwhelming numbers.

As Sergeant Messmer leaned against the wooden planks, he began to shake.

"We're lucky to be alive," stated Sergeant Watson, who sat next to him. "Total carnage. Bodies just exploded into pieces. Just like shooting melons. Their innards just hung from them."

"None of us were heroes," Sergeant Messmer stated, "not for this. We did what we had to do. Good thing; the Lieutenant surrendered. Emotions overwhelmed my reasoning. I never want to be considered a hero.

We just did our job." He paused for a moment, and then said, "I was almost killed a few times."

"No reason to die for nothing. We're safe, now. Until we're liberated, we relax in a P.O.W. camp. Let the others fight."

Sergeant Messmer smiled, and then said, "We sure kicked them in their rumps." He then chuckled, before saying, "We showed 'um. The only choice was to kill or be killed."

"That'll teach 'um." Sergeant Watson said, as he smiled. "All were scared. That's expected. When our boys are backed into a corner, they showed their stuff. Good bunch."

The door opened and a few Germans entered with crackers and cheese. The men moved away from them as they placed the food on a table. Each man walked past the area and was given a portion.

"Smells nasty, stated Private Branson. He checked all his pockets, before saying, "Dirty Krauts took everything."

"I don't have anything, either," said a younger soldier behind him.

"Army food seems good, now," Private Branson said, as he glanced toward the others. "What kind of cheese is this?"

"Don't know," said the younger soldier.

"My luck. Probably rotten."

"You guys had it rough?" the younger soldier asked.

"Rough? You don't know what rough is," he said, as he sat by a beam. "What's your name?"

"Bill Mead," he replied, as he sat next to the Private and then began to eat a the crackers.

A rat moved past their feet.

"Boy, those Krauts just keep coming. We used grenades, bazookas, rifles, M-1's, flamethrowers, and machine guns. We used everything. We mowed 'um down. There must have been about 100 or more Krauts killed in our area. As more fell, more came. We held 'um off about all day, until we retreated. Many of them were just as scared, as we were. Some trembled as they raised their weapons. Some were so frightened; they were petrified. Easy targets. Most were hardened soldiers. A few were just old men and kids. The master race bleeds, like everyone else." He momentarily glanced toward the cheese, broke it, and then tears appeared, before he said, "Just total madness." He looked toward the younger soldier, and then said, "What happened with your unit?"

"We surrendered in one of the smaller towns. Their tanks were approaching. We had no chance, so we lifted our hands, and then walked into the road."

"You could have been killed."

"Maybe so," said Mead. "All of us were just office personnel. They gave us rifles and told us to fight. I was so scared. I saw too many of the others die. We had no chance."

"None of us did, kid."

Mead smiled, and stated, "I was aiming at one of the Krauts, behind the tank. I was sweating and then I began to shake. I couldn't shoot. None of us could."

"It's over son. When the war is over, you'll be back home."

"How long?"

"Hard to say," replied Corporal Branson. "We'll just have to bear it, until they're defeated."

106

He tasted the cheese, and then said, "Tastes pitiful. Definitely spoiled."

"My parents will be worried."

"So will my wife," Corporal Branson said, before he ate a cracker.

"Married long?" asked Mead, as he tasted the cheese.

"About three years, he replied, before continuing to eat.

After the younger soldier frowned, he asked, "Good wife?"

He swallowed the food, before replying, "The best. None better. I never will know why she wanted me." He paused, and then said, "Maybe, I do. We have many of the same personality traits. We always understood each other."

"I hope that I find someone like that someday," Mead said.

"Always treat woman, like roses. They smell sweet and are beautiful to look at, but just watch out for the thorns."

The kid laughed, and said, "Good advice."

"You sure; you're eighteen, Mead?" More crackers and cheese were consumed. "You look awfully young."

"I volunteered on my eighteenth birthday. I wanted to fight. In basic, I was given a desk job." He ate a piece of cheese. "Just too klutzy."

"You better be, kid. I saw a few booted out for lying about their age. There are limits. Hitler has an excuse."

The fighting still continued with the defenders of St Vith, which was a vital crossroads for the Germans. The 9th armored division and the 112th infantry supported the

106th within the city. The enemy was relentless with their attack. More came and the pressure increased but the advance was postponed until the troops were ordered to withdraw to the west.

American tanks, artillery, and armored cars were initially used.

The soldiers, who were killed, wounded in action, missing, or taken prisoner were 89,500 during the entire aggression.

The army was segregated during World War II. During the Battle of the Bulge, many black people served. All were honorable men but they weren't recognized for their service during the conflict.

One artillery unit was the 333rd. The Negro soldiers helped fire the guns. Their location was many miles from the front. When they were overwhelmed, they stayed to stop the Germans. Most were killed but others escaped. The rest were eventually found by the SS and massacred.

Another unit was the 761st Tank Battalion. These men landed at Normandy, helped the 3rd armored division and were the first in Morville-les-vic, and Tillet. The Germans were defeated and the towns freed from tyranny with their sacrifice. Other units always took credit for their victories.

Red was everyone's blood with different nationalities and races.

The weather, unsanitary conditions, and poor diet from the march and in the barn caused problems. A few men died from their wounds and fatigue. Others became sick with fever and diarrhea. As the days progressed, some of the men became weaker.

Sergeant Messmer and the others rested. He awoke and looked toward the man next to him. After touching his shoulder, no movement was seen. He had no more life. Weakness from his wounds and the elements caused his demise.

Even if the battle was over, death continued. The struggle for life never ended. The men were still in danger from the elements. If the situation didn't improve, more would die.

"Hey, this man is dead!" shouted Sergeant Messmer/ "He's dead!"

Another soldier turned toward the Sergeant, as a few others checked the body.

"Poor fellow," said a soldier. "Not an honorable death."

Sergeant Messmer gazed upon him with disgust.

One of the Americans informed the German guards.

After checking the body, they allowed two prisoners to bury the man. After the dog tags were removed, the men began to dig through the snow into the partially frozen ground. Two guards watched the men, as the hole became larger. The body was eventually placed into the grave and the dirt and snow thrown over the body.

"When will be taken from the stink hole!" yelled a soldier, as the watched through a window.

As they waited, the other men were becoming restless.

"Sarge," said Rayburn, "we'll all die, like him. The only plan for anyone is death."

"No," he said, as he turned toward the man. "Don't lose hope. There's nothing; we can do. The fight for survival continues. No one will face death alone. Remember your words. The will of God will be revealed for each one of us."

Both stood by the rear stalls.

Rayburn stated, "With all our strength, we must survive."

"Did you hear anything about our wounded?" asked the Sergeant.

"Nothing, after we surrendered," he replied. "I wouldn't trust any of the Krauts. Rumors are circulating; unarmed prisoners were killed."

"If we knew, all of us would have died fighting," the Sergeant said. "Using our bear hands and bayonets was more honorable, than dying defenseless."

"What's better a quick death or a slow torture?"

"As long as we live, there's a chance," replied Sergeant Messmer. "Always have hope. Since we weren't killed, the Lieutenant made the correct decision. There were too many of them for us to handle, anyway."

"Maybe, so," said Rayburn. "God has everything planned."

"God knows everyone's limits. I will not question his will. Why do some die and others live? There is no discrimination from a bullet or shrapnel. Anyone could die at anytime. Is it luck or something else?"

Both men just stared toward each other.

"None of us are heroes," said the Sarge. "I performed my duty to protect my men and myself. We fought to survive. I didn't like what I had to do, but it had to be done, and I never will regret it."

"If I ever see Hitler, I'd shoot him," said Rayburn. "Not too Christian of me. If killing him, prevents more death, I'd do it. Too many good men were lost."

"Killing him a million times won't change anything. God has a plan for him, also. Nothing will change God's will."

"Go ahead and throw my words back at me."

"No matter how or when he dies, God will be waiting," the Sarge stated. "We must continue to pray, even if no results are seen. If I ever get out of this nightmare, I want to really know the true God."

"How does anyone know him?" asked Rayburn. "By doing what he would do."

"Anyone can imitate his deeds," the Sergeant replied. "Good deeds don't mean anything. How does a relationship exist with God?"

Many men were marched to Geroelstein. More boxcars and engines were needed. The mass surrenders weren't anticipated. Before the men were transported, facilities needed to be prepared for the prisoners.

Adjustments needed to be made for the influx.

The battle changed all the men. The world could never be viewed as it was. The days, which were behind them, were over, and the days, which faced each one, were just beginning. The scares were permanent. Many of the survivors developed a respect for others and a love of life, which no one else could understand. The horror was only experienced by the few throughout history, who saw the fragility of life, and developed a special understanding.

"This place makes me sick," said a soldier. "We're all going to die in this rat hole."

"Rick, there's nothing; we can do," said the other man.

"If we are taken deeper inside Germany, we'll have no chance. Now is the time to act."

"There's no place to go, Joel?" he asked.

"We can head toward the woods. They won't waste their time with us. Well wait, until it's dark. Some of these rotten slats can easily be broken."

"What about the others?"

"Too many will be a risk," stated Joel Overston. The two of us will succeed. If our bodies become too weak, we have no chance."

The other man glanced toward the wall and then tounched the wood, before saying, "What time?"

"The guards are changed every four hours. We'll wait, until about Midnight. Their complacency may give us an edge. If our timing is right, we'll make it."

"We should rest and conserve our strength."

"Nothing else we can to do anyway."

Captain Grant was brought with the next batch of men.

His stature was still impressive. No one could deny his authority. The battle caused him to weary and frustrated. Images of the battle within his thoughts gave him grief.

The outcome to him was inevitable. The massive nature of the attack was a challenge. It was impossible to overcome without a superior counter attack from the Allies, which wasn't ready to occur. Military intelligence needed more information and proper planning to defeat the German forces.

The Captain was proud of all his men, even if he thought that some deserted him. His force was scattered and the pockets of resistance didn't have the strength of the whole. Nothing could have prevented the result.

The determination of his men and others caused the Germans to deploy resources and waste time. Their plan was delayed, which gave him much satisfaction, as more information was acquired. Their rears were kicked and the enemy suffered from their determination. He would have preferred dying with his men but surrender, even though a humiliation was the only option.

Sacrificing his life for nothing was unacceptable.

The reinforcements never arrived and his men fought until there was no hope of survival. Many wanted to continue.

As Sergeant Messmer, others became obsessed with the moment. Some pleaded for the Captain to surrender and called him foul-mouthed words, which greatly angered and displeased his sensibilities.

He wanted to continue and hold his position, but the strength of the enemy was not known. All of them would have been killed. The Captain had no choice and finally relented, when he saw no hope of survival.

The Captain never forgot the attitude of the men.

None of the men understood the reasoning for his determination and vigor. He was their commander and the military manual was his bible. In his mind, everything had to be done by the book. Rules needed to be obeyed and authority exerted for discipline. His decisions were final. The others just obeyed orders, even if all had the possibility of being killed.

The barn was becoming overcrowded with about 100 prisoners. The Captain talked to various men and then walked toward Sergeant Messmer.

"Messmer!" he shouted. "What happened to you?"

"A.W.O.L.," stated the Sergeant, as he saluted and then smiled.

The Captain disgustingly returned the salute, before saying, "Don't be a smart mouth. Your squad?" he asked, as he noticed his coat. "You had it rough?"

"Same as the rest. We held 'um for as long as possible."

"Too bad about Waller. Good man."

"Yes, sir."

After pausing for a moment, the Captain said, "Good job, Sergeant. How do you access our situation?"

"For now, dismal. We're waiting to be transported. Maybe, conditions will improve, after the men are processed."

"Encourage your men. Never lose hope. Survive at all costs."

A salute was given.

The gesture was returned, before the Sergeant stated, "Thank you, sir."

The Captain walked into the distance as couple of men walked toward the Sergeant.

114

"Good man," Corporal Smith stated.

"Too pompous for my tastes," said Jefferson.

"Watch it," said the Sergeant. "He has his purpose. Have respect."

"Staying inside the pillbox," Jefferson stated, "while the men were being slaughtered, was not acceptable to many of us."

Corporal Smith replied, "One more man would have made no difference."

"He should have bleed with us," said Jefferson. "Staying in the pillbox, when the snow and trees was soaked in blood, was a disgrace." He looked toward his hands, and then said, "They'll never be clean."

"We do what we're told," said the Sergeant. "If he wants us to kill, we kill to survive. If he wants us to die, we die. It is not our job to question orders. The past is over. Nothing can change what happened. All of us have to accept authority and the privileges of his position."

"Bullets ripped bodies to shreds." Jefferson stated. "'Blasts severed limbs. People on both sides cried for help. Blood splashed everywhere and squirted from bodies. Will the cries for help ever leave my mind and the blood wash from my hands?"

"Live with it!" shouted the Sergeant, as he grabbed the man's jacket. "Nothing can change what happened." Before releasing his grip, he said, "We had no choice. If we didn't kill, we'd be dead. Do you hear what I am saying? 'We worry about now. Think about every moment, until we are dead or back home. Do you hear me?"

115

Both nodded.

"No one knows what awaits us. I'm as scared as everyone else. Just accept what life has to offer. I want out of here, like everyone else, but there's nothing; we can do. Just thank God; we're alive."

The battle still continued in many areas.

As reinforcements arrived throughout the area, the enemy continued to exhaust fuel and ammunition.

The prisoners spent one night in the barn. The daylight was decreasing. The next day was December the 20th. Everyone was becoming more irritated. They were only fed once. Especially with the rumors of executions, trust for the Germans was nonexistent.

A couple of others died and were buried.

Hope was decreasing for a positive outcome.

Two men were ready to initiate their plan. They waited, as the hours passed. If they succeeded, they would leave the death trap. As the guards passed the wall from various directions, proper timing was essential. Noise had to be kept to a minimum. If they could run into the trees without detection, no one would realize their absence, until morning.

Two men peered through the planks of the barn.

After the guard passed their position, the boards on the outer wall were carefully removed. The wood broke easily with very little noise. The snow was removed to give them enough room to squeeze through the small opening. They replaced the board, as another guard walked a few feet from the wall.

As the guard turned the corner, the boards were removed and then they quickly squeezed through the opening. They began to run into the distance as the rest of the men slept. Their tracks would easily be visible in the snow at daylight, but they continued, and entered the woods.

Their senses were overwhelmed by fear.

Weapons fire awoke the men. One of the guards noticed the escape and fired toward the men. Both were hit and killed. The noise awoke many of the men, but none knew what happened, until the morning, when two more graves were dug.

More German soldiers arrived from town and helped prepare the prisoners for the next phase of their journey.

The men were asked to leave the barn and assembly in front of the building.

"About time," many of the men said.

"We're out of here," stated Private Branson, as he lifted himself from the floor.

"Anything has to be better than this infestation," said Little Joe, as he walked toward the others. "Too many rats and other vermin."

The men looked miserable.

All needed a shave. No beards were evident but the outcome was inevitable without proper grooming. They were dirty and their clothes soiled. The odor was disgusting from their clothes and bodies.

Some were sick from the elements.

The men began to walk outside and stand in formation. They were told by one of them, who could speak English; they had nothing to fear, if they cooperated. Time was of the essence to board them on the train.

Once in Bad Orb, many of the detainees from various trains, including men from the 106th and 28th infantry division would be processed at the neighboring prison camp. Unknown to many of the men, the journey continued for the ones, who were less fortunate to other areas of Germany.

Stalag IX-B couldn't handle the influx of all the prisoners.

The men were asked to state their names, rank, and serial numbers.

Eventually, they were walked from the outskirts of town to the train depot. This was a main hub for railroad line. Before being transported to Bad Orb, some waited to board the boxcars within warehouses. Before boarding, others waited outside. Relief was apparent on their faces. The experiences of the barn were no longer relevant.

The journey toward their ultimate destination continued. The unknown still frightened them. The path was not their choice. No one knew the outcome. Every movement toward their future could cause death. They were at the mercy of the Germans.

No one had control of fate.

Men were divided into groups for transport.

The 40 by 8 boxcars could be used for, at most, eight horses, supplies, and ammunition, plus other needs.

They held 40 men in a standing position but more prisoners, usually at most 60, were placed inside the wooden enclosures. Only a

118

little straw was on the floor. There were no windows or heat within the boxcars. Sometimes, slight gaps exited between the planks. The sanitation was an individual's helmet. All were squeezed together and miserable.

Only body warmth sustained them.

The transport times varied, after arriving at Geroelstein. No one knew, when the men were to depart to Bad Orb. The Germans just seemed to randomly choose certain groups or individuals and place them within the boxcars. As more prisoners arrived, some departed, and others waited, until transportation was available to Bad Orb or other locations within Germany.

Anxiety increased as their relief from their previous experiences was diminished.

Many hours were needed for everyone to be loaded on a specific train. Each man stepped a metal ledge and then walked into the container until no more room existed. While they waited for the other boxcars to be filled, more time expired in the almost total darkness. More than one train left the station at various intervals, as others prisoners waited to be loaded.

Chapter Six: The Boxcar

As time progressed, the men from Company F were randomly loaded into various boxcars with the men from other units. Each one entered and was pushed to the rear. After the door was closed, darkness was upon them. As other containers were filled, they waited.

Until no more space existed, the prisoners were continually squeezed into the enclosures.

There was no room to move. Bodies pushed against one other. Their breath could be seen between them. All stood within close proximity. Relaxation was nonexistent. None could sit on the floor without disturbing the others.

These same types of boxcars were used to transport Jewish prisoners to concentration camps. The conditions of transport were basically the same for everyone. Certain groups had no use within the Nazis plan for domination. All had their destinations for life or death.

The journeys for everyone began in darkness within a wooden box.

Train whistles and the pressure from the steam were heard. The odor from the engine was prevalent. From the utterances of the Germans and the other prisoners, they knew; their departure was postponed. Much noise penetrated the walls. When the noise receded, the next phase began.

None could find comfort

The trains usually took about 4 days to travel to Bad Orb. The men were not allowed to leave the boxcars to stretch their legs, even if the train stopped to change the guard or for the needs of the engine. No food was given to most of the men on different trains during the trip, but water was available. If some food was given, the men were given their share at the beginning of the trip. Day travel was limited, especially when the skies cleared to prevent attacks from the Allied planes.

The trip didn't require four days under normal conditions. The route was too close to the front, so precautions were necessary. The snow was also causing problems on the tracks. Other trains may have encountered problems and slowed progression. The train traveled at a slower pace because of the weather. Stops were needed for the engines to be refilled with water. Time was of the essence, but many issues, caused the delay.

If the train stopped, the men found no comfort. None were allowed to leave the boxcars. The situation may have varied for others during the transport. The experience was horrifying. Infection and diarrhea were the main results at the end of the journey.

The trip began and the men felt the vibrations. The train slowly left the train depot. As the speed increased, the boxcar occasionally jerked. The men swayed from the vibrations. All held each other on occasion and the walls to support each other and prevent injuries.

Christmas was arriving and many of the men thought of better times.

The snow on the countryside was beautiful and pristine.

The train traveled southwest toward Bad Orb. The war was behind the men. As the train continued, the violence was becoming less of a factor within their minds.

The light from the sun was becoming less prevalent. The black engine and dark brown boxcars cast shadows in the snow. From a distance, no one knew the cargo of the trains. Surface appearances were deceiving. The smoke from the stack contrasted with the picturesque view.

As the shadows increased, the light faded and the darkness was revealed.

Hatches did exist on the upper sections of the boxcar. These were used by the Germans but not for prisoners, especially during the winter months. Three existed on each side, which slid down on wooden tracks.

Two were in the front and one in the back. The dimensions were about 2 feet by 3 feet. The panels were secure so the men would not escape.

"Sarge, at least we're on the move," Corporal Conroy disgustingly said.

"Just don't give up hope," Sergeant Messmer replied. Don't worry about tomorrow. It'll come soon enough."

The train whistle blew.

Conversations of other men were occasionally heard. The men talked about different interests. While they spoke, the anxiety was relieved.

When they communicated, time elapsed more quickly.

As words were exchanged, the anguish was diminished and momentarily forgotten.

The Corporal stated, "The war is over for us." Another soldier bumped into him, before he continued by saying, "I've seen some photographs. Germany is a beautiful country."

"If we could see it," the Sergeant said, as he tried to glance through the intersections of the boards. "Nothing can be seen." He turned toward the man. "Your parents have a big Christmas, Jim?"

"Not really. My mom cooks just for my dad and me. She spends hours in the kitchen and we finish the meal, so quickly. What about your family?"

With my brothers and sisters, the meal is an event," The Sergeant replied. "We have a beautiful Christmas tree and nice gifts. My parents aren't rich, but during the holidays happiness and blessings come."

"How many?"

"4 brothers and 3 sisters. One brother died, when he was young. Jake's an altar boy. He's the youngest at 10 years. He loves the Catholic Church. I'm not too faithful."

"You don't go to church too much."

"No, just during special events," said the Sergeant. "Too stuffy."

"I try to attend every week."

"What denomination are you?" the Sergeant asked.

"Baptist."

"That's right. I remember. You told me at Camp Atterbury."

"Not like the Catholic church," stated the Corporal.

"Well, the authority of the Catholic church is impressive with solid roots toward St. Peter and Jesus."

"Yes," said the Corporal, "on this rock, I'll build my church. Means different things to some people."

"Too many have left the Catholic faith, since the beginnings. The ultimate authority will always be the Pope, a representation of Jesus. God speaks through him." The Sergeant paused, and then regretfully said, "He just seems so far away and impersonal. Everything seems so high and mighty. With the ceremony and formality, the Pope seems so out of touch from everyday problems. I just don't know why things happen. During the battle, I could have been killed. Why was I spared, while others died?"

"Everyone has to believe in God, when death approaches. You wanted to stay and fight. I had enough killing. A few of the German soldiers weren't trained properly. As they walked toward us, they were horrified. This war is not for the young boys or the old men. They were killed with the most horrifying expressions. I had to shoot them. Why didn't God protect them?"

"It was them or us," Sergeant Messmer said. "All had weapons and grenades. They were ready to die for their cause. If we didn't kill them, they would have killed us. No other factors were relevant." He glanced toward his coat, and then said, "Bullet holes and shredded. It's Impossible to comprehend. Is it luck or the hand of God? Maybe, I'll understand someday."

"If we survive," stated the Corporal.

The Sergeant frowned and then stared toward him for a few moments, before staying, "Is anyone else from our squad in this freezer?"

"I didn't see anyone else when we entered. I saw a few of the men enter the other boxcars."

The Sergeant rubbed his hands on his arms, smiled, and then said, "Just a cold hell."

"In a way, Sarge, everyone has their own hell."

"Maybe so, but burning or freezing for eternity is not what I want. How long is this ride?"

Another man replied, "About four days. I overheard the Germans. We're traveling, cautiously. We should arrive by Christmas Eve."

"You understand German?" said Corporal Conroy.

The other man responded by saying, "Somewhat. I was raised in an area with people, who spoke the language."

"When the weather clears, the air force will finish those Krauts," said the Sergeant. "The battle is not over."

"Isn't Messmer of German heritage?" asked the other man.

"Yes it is," the Sergeant replied. "The name was Messimer. It was changed after my

125

relatives came to America. Too many people discriminated against certain backgrounds during those times." He momentarily paused, and then told him, "We win this war by killing Krauts. If more of them die, more Americans live. They don't represent the heritage of my grandfather. Many hardships were encountered, after he arrived in America. I suppose that times change." He aggressively stared toward him, before asking, "Want to make something of it that I am partly of German heritage? With your wimpy chicken legs, no one would care."

The man became angry, and then said, "Good thing; you're a Sergeant or I'd bust you in the mouth."

"Just try it!" yelled the Sergeant.

Some of the other men told them to be quite.

"Never mind, Sarge," replied the soldier. "The Nazis Party doesn't represent my heritage either. I don't want any trouble."

"We're not here to fight each other," said the Corporal.

"All that's important is what comes from within," the Sergeant stated. "Labels mean nothing."

"What do you think those Nazi prison camps are like?" asked the Corporal.

Sergeant Messmer replied, "No sense worrying, until we know. The German prisoners were given steak and potatoes. I doubt, if we will be so lucky. He smiled, before saying, "Just enjoy the ride."

"Until the next hell," said Corporal Conroy.

The Sergeant chuckled.

Memories surfaced of the battle. Explosions were still heard within the Sergeants thoughts. The violence bothered him. The Sergeant knew his duty was to protect himself and his squad. The bloody images and cries from the wounded were seen and heard.

The carnage was horrifying to his mind, like many others.

Memories needed to be released and the conflict resolved.

Their engine carried about 10 boxcars of prisoners. The amount for each train varied, which depended on different factors, like boxcar availability and processing concerns with the influx of prisoners. A caboose was attached, which contained the guards. The engine proceeded with caution. During stops, in most cases the prisoners were not unloaded.

Not enough water was available within each boxcar for the needs of the men.

While being confined without proper ventilation, health problems began to surface.

Food was not supplied to the ones on this train. Other prisoners were feed only once. Before the departure, they were given a piece of bread and a little cheese. The lack of nutrition was causing the wounded and the healthy to become weaker.

Christmas was approaching in a few days and despite the hardships, the memories continued to surface of happier times. When the train was parked, the men sometimes began to sing holiday songs. The distraction was needed to relieve the pressure. Certain songs were requested by some men, which uplifted everyone's spirits.

As one began to sing, others followed, until almost all participated.

The German guards didn't interfere. The guards heard the prisoners without emotion. Within the dilemma, hope flourished of a greater purpose. The season was upon all of them for hope and joy. Their troubles were suppressed for the moment but always within their thoughts. The singing relieved the tensions and reminded them of happier times. Even as prisoners, they knew; a higher authority was in control of their destiny.

The few, who died on the journey, were not removed from the train.

The weather and overcast skies were still a burden. The war was fought with ground forces until the skies began to clear on the 23rd of December. The men, who had access to more ammunition and food, held their positions in many of the cities. Reinforcements were arriving at a slow pace, which was due to the weather and other factors.

The defenders of St. Vith were forced to retreat to the Salm River. The delay caused many problems for the plans of the aggressors.

The environmental conditions were still harsh for everyone. Snow was everywhere. With the lack of proper nutrition and environmental factors, the weakest perished. A few couldn't withstand the elements with their wounds or other aliments. The battle was completed, but the anguish continued.

As Christmas approached, the men continued to sing.

None could observe the countryside from the boxcars during various stopovers.

The scene was serine and unscarred by war. All the landscape was covered in snow, which hid the underlying reality. Much of the terrain was farmland, and hillier areas with trees and lakes. The wind sometimes blew, which caused the flakes to glide over the snow.

Although the time of the holidays was upon them, the contrasts of peace and war were disturbing and conflicting to their thought processes.

Military personnel were on the roads. Canvas trucks, equipment, and men were traveling west toward the front. The Nazis offensive was continuing. All of them knew, when the sky cleared, planes would destroy the German supply lines and military targets. Supplies could be dropped to the defenders.

The advantage would shift toward the allies.

None of the men knew the truth of what was happening on the front.

The Germans, who spoke English, implied; the battle was continuing and within their grasp was a victorious outcome. Their men were pushing west and the Allies were being easily defeated. The cities were falling and the Third Reich was reestablishing their territories. The Americans were being pushed into the sea and humiliated.

Some men became so agitated during the journey a few arguments erupted. Tensions were high and moral low. All tried to forget the past.

With Christmas approaching, most concentrated on happier memories. The scars of battle and their uncertain future caused occasionally eruptions of violence. A few of the men's behavior became irrational.

On some of the trains, there were a few escape attempts by the prisoners, if an opportunity arose. None had a chance. The Germans killed these men without hesitation. Others stepped on land minds.

Their location was unfamiliar.

With the snow and frigid weather conditions, there was nowhere to run and hide.

Desperation overwhelmed their senses.

The boxcars had little hay and no room on the floor existed to sit down. The excrement from various animals was within the boxcars. The enclosure was very disgusting and smelled like a stink pit.

The conditions were unhealthy.

When the men needed relief, a few helmets were used. If cracks between the floorboards existed, the waste was drained toward the tracks. The sanitary conditions were nonexistent. The odor and smell continued to increase during the trip and was sickening. No one was allowed to leave the train, when the train stopped.

Unhealthy conditions caused much distress.

As the men fought for survival, the horrifying journey continued.

Many trains were proceeding toward Bad Orb from Geroelstein and other areas. Locomotives were on the same track. Because of various hazards, caution was used to proceed toward their destination. The German guards were in constant communication with the other trains. The transport of the men was handled with efficiency, even with the harsh conditions.

While the captives were being transported, the battle raged.

As more information was gathered, the truth was exposed. Reinforcements were needed. The invasion was being evaluated, while supplies and men were being prepared. The influx of personnel was increasing, which was appreciated by the weary troops.

The process wasn't immediate and the weather conditions caused problems.

The Allies increased their strength from about 83,000 men on the day of the attack to about 610,000 on December 23. These new recruits and the supply lines of the Allies were crucial to stop the advance. The resistance increased, which caused the Germans to waste fuel, ammunition, and supplies.

At Bastogne on the same day, when the weather cleared, a parachute drop was initiated. The survivors, held their positions, as the cities crumbled. Tanks and extra troops were sent toward the city. The process was tedious and slow, but help was arriving.

Many cities, which were vigorously defended, needed supplies.

Prisoners from various units were processed in many locations.

The destination of the captives on the train was a prison camp. All thought that their journey ended at Bad Orb. Stalag IX-B was on the outskirts of the city. This was the processing center for the 106th prisoners and others. The problem was; only a certain amount could be handled.

Some trains would continue to other camps, which were in various locations within Germany. Space was limited and overcrowding occurred at all facilities. The Germans used their best judgment to assign the captives. No planning was properly initiated for the enormous inundation. An enormous quantity of men needed to be processed and detained.

The amount was just too overwhelming to prevent problems. Conditions at the prison camps were becoming more horrific. Nothing could solve the problems. The Germans did not consider these camps a high priority. Sacrifices needed to implement, especially with the embargos.

As another day passed, others died within the boxcars.

"Only a few more hours," said Corporal Conroy, "and we should be arriving in Bad Orb."

Sergeant Messmer stated, "About time. I've had it."

"We'll arrive the day, before Christmas," the Corporal said. "Still a good time of year."

"Sure is," said the soldier, who spoke with them, earlier. "I heard one of the Germans say, yesterday, during the stop to fill the engine; the sky's were clearing."

"About time," stated the Corporal. "Our air force can do their job, now. Hitler had the advantage for a while."

"No chance for their pilots," Sergeant Messmer stated.

"I feel more warmth," said the Corporal. "Even with the sun, it's still too cold."

The Sergeant stated, "This time of year is my favorite." After pausing, he continued, "No matter what the condition of the prison camp, we'll be better off. I can't take this, anymore."

"Only the birth of the Savior sustains me. His sacrifice was much worse."

"Is Jesus watching over us?" asked the Sergeant.

"He watches over everyone."

After smiling, the Sergeant stated, "No doubt. We're in his hands. If we pray, he will hear us."

The Corporal nodded, and then said, "The prison camp will be a blessing to this misery. Everyone should rejoice."

"Be grateful for what we do have during the holidays, even if this train is not even worth a 2nd class ticket."

Both laughed.

The Sergeant and Corporal followed the example of a few others, who began to sing a Christmas carol.

Most sang to suppress the violence and death, which encompassed them. Jesus was born and died for everyone. Life and death was within his grasp. Even if they were killed, no one could destroy their souls. If they believed, their destination was secure with him for eternity. No one could diminish anyone's will to live. They were sustained by the love of God.

Jesus was the true God, and the Savior for everyone, including the Germans. The will of Jesus was not forced on anyone. He was followed by choice. No intimidation was needed. Only by love, he ruled with a firm hand. Everyone must choose the correct path for his love to flourish.

The train continued toward Bad Orb.

The men were pleased; the journey was about to end. The condition of the prison camp was not an issue. The horror of being confined within the walls of the boxcar was unimaginable. Except for those men, no one could understand.

They were humiliated and treated like animals.

Although many of the men tried to lift the spirits of the others by talking and singing, the truth of their confinement wasn't overcome. The guards were untrustworthy. Any of the men could be killed by the Germans or die from the elements. Because their future was uncertain, the men were scared.

As the train entered the train yard of Bad Orb, the men became more optimistic. Christmas was the next day and the thoughts of the holidays overwhelmed any fears. All other emotions were suppressed. The thoughts of their families and happier times became prevalent. The ones, who survived, were safe. A prison camp was the next step. The war was still raging, but they were removed from the violence, as they proceeded further inside Germany.

As the men smiled, they sang more Christmas songs.

Everything was peaceful and quite outside the boxcar.

They were blessed and happy to survive the horrors of war. Nothing could be worse than the battle and their journey. They had confidence that the war would be easily won by the Allies. The amount of time for their confinement would be very minor. They knew; all of them would eventually be rescued from their imprisonment. As they waited safely within the prison camp, others would continue the fight.

Freedom was within their thoughts and the final destination.

All prayed for the war to end.

Until liberation came to all the ones, who were suppressed, none would be satisfied. Everyone's life seemed more important and respect was increasing for everyone. No one saw the world, as they did. What each one experienced was personal and never could be explained. All knew something; others would never know. War was not the final judgment for the oppressors.

Life and death was so fragile.

The love of man was not the love of God. A person's true heart expressed the truth. Love came in many forms. Whether any acts were obviously wrong or acceptable to the masses, the Spirit of God was the deciding factor. If the love came from above and entered everyone's heart, all, who accepted the Savior, would live without fear and be at peace.

Humanity brought sulfuring to the world. No policies brought true peace and happiness. Nothing was perfect and the domino effect always prevailed. While some prospered, others were suppressed. Groups gained power and others were downgraded. People gained monetary stature while others lost their wealth. Change has improved everyone's life but never brought inner peace.

The spirit of man needed to be replaced by the Spirit of God. The true love of God was necessary for everyone. Good works wasn't the answer to demonstrate holiness. Too many competed with others to signify their relationship with his will.

With the proper guidance, all were equal and righteous. The deeds of humanity caused good or evil. A pure heart manifested neither of these attributes. The requirements from God were a change in demeanor from an inner peace. If a person manifested the gifts, good works weren't necessary to profess righteousness. All actions were pleasing to his will and used for goodness, if the true word of God guided the believers.

By force, the war would be won by the Allies and the world restored to peace. Evil has always resurfaced in many forms. Maybe, this was the war to end all wars. Men have always fought and defended the rights of others to prevent tyranny. The men were only concerned with their safety and returning home.

When the war was over, they would be satisfied, and return home with honor and pride for their survival against the tyranny of the Third Reich.

Peace and joy would return to everyone.

As they sang, the sound of sirens was heard. The song decreased, as each man began to focus on the occurrence. Except for the warning, silence became prevalent. Nothing else was heard within the boxcar for the moment.

The pause of silence seemed eternal.

"Air raid!" shouted Sergeant Messmer and a few of the other men.

The men stared toward the ceiling.

"Let us out!" screamed a few, as they pounded on the door. "Help! Let us out!"

An American plane was flying toward the train yard. The pilot saw an opportunity to destroy the supply lines of the Third Reich. Attacking ammunition and reinforcements would avenge the deaths of his brothers.

His objective was clear and mind focused.

He began his decent and was ready to attack. The time was within his grasp to retaliate for the invasion. As the boxcars were targeted within the sensors, the pressure on the trigger from his finger increased.

An oxygen mask was over mouth. Sweat was visible on his forehead. He did not hesitate, as he dissented. The noise from the engine and the air passing the wings caused a buzzing sound.

The sound increased, which caused the fear of the prisoners to amplify. All knew what was happening. Nothing could be done, except yell for help. The screams increased, as a few of the men began to kick the door.

The pilot pushed a button and dropped a bomb, which exploded in the train yard.

The German soldiers and civilians were running for cover. Some ran into shelters. Others ran into buildings. A few jumped into foxholes. Others dove under the trains. There was no place of safety, if a bomb exploded or bullets impacted their domains. Until the threat was no longer present, hiding was the only alternative.

Weapons were fired from defensive positions. Anti-aircraft bombs exploded in the sky. Machine guns were used. Streaks of light could be seen shooting toward the attacker. As the plane descended, the German soldiers held their position. The prisoners weren't their concern. They were defending themselves and the residents of the city.

Since none of the guards responded, the men within the various boxcars tired to kick open their doors.

Boxcars were everywhere within the train yard. They were parked on sidetracks and on the main line. All were filled with prisoners from the front. All were targets for annihilation.

Bullets were fired from the plane.

As the bullets penetrated the walls of a few boxcars, including the one with Sergeant Messmer, without warning, the men fell toward the floor.

Some of the soldiers groaned.

Sergeant Messmer pushed a man off his body, who was shot in the back and killed. He did not know the man. A stranger saved his life with luck or by divine intervention. His thoughts were confused. One died to save another. He couldn't comprehend the reasoning. None had to be killed, if there was a God, but since there is a God, why was he spared.

A few of the men and Sergeant Messmer banged on the walls and yelled for help. Some continued to kick the door. Others pushed and cried for help. No one seemed to hear the cries. No mercy was shown toward them, as they continued their efforts.

A few helped the injured. A bullet penetrated the helmet of another man in another boxcar, which knocked him unconscious. He was fine, but a few others were injured or killed. The men used anything available to stop the bleeding of the wounded.

No hope existed for a couple of the men.

The violence was just random. Destiny wasn't controlled by anyone. The reasoning why some died and others lived was unclear to all the men. Only a couple of boxcars were hit. Most of the men were not hurt by the attack. Bullets and shrapnel weren't meant for any specific person. These projectiles impacted anything in their path.

A noise was heard at the door. Someone was trying to unlock it. The door slide open and one of the German guards yelled, "Snell!"

Other men were still trapped, but within a few boxcars, the men succeeded to break the doors, and then many began to run for cover, as the plane returned. They didn't know the area, but instinct prevailed. All wanted to live. Any cover was used to hide from the relentless attack. Some men were hesitant to leave the boxcars.

After Sergeant Messmer exited, he yelled toward the men to make a P.O.W. sign with their bodies in the snow.

The plane shot toward the men. Bullets impacted the ground. Others were killed, as they ran. As a few men ran toward a small hill in the distance, panic was in their faces. All began to lie in the proper positions.

A few other Sergeants screamed for a P.O.W. sign.

Sergeant Messmer looked toward the sky, and then screamed. "Stupid pilot!" He then ran toward the hill and helped the others.

"Make a P.O.W. sign!" others yelled, as they exited the boxcars.

"If I had a gun, I'd shoot him out of the sky," said Staff Sergeant Barker. "We're Americans!" he yelled toward the plane. "Nearsighted jackass!"

A few of the men dragged the wounded off the platforms.

Before the sign was completed, a few other Sergeants jumped into the snow with the other men, to complete the message.

The plane, as it was about to fire, noticed them.

After realizing his mistake from their heroic efforts, he tipped the wings a few times, and then flew into the distance.

The pilot bowed his head and was regretful. As he began to think of what happened, tears eventually appeared on his face. His hand began to shake for a few moments on the throttle. For as long as he lived, the incident was never forgotten. After the war, there were rumors; the pilot committed suicide.

Other pilots committed the same acts at other train yards. The incident was common. The British and American pilots were too anxious and their targets were misinterpreted. No one could blame them for their enthusiasm and courage. All regretted their error of judgment and suffered the consequences with their memories of the incidents.

The men lifted themselves from the snow and cheered.

The men followed military procedure and won the battle with wisdom.

The Germans and Americans watched the plane fly into the distance and were relieved. The ones, who hid themselves, reappeared. All were shaken with the incident. The memories of this Christmas Eve were never forgotten.

While the war continued, there was no peace for anyone.

The train with Sergeant Messmer and the others pulled out toward the prison camp, the next day. Most of the men from the 106th and some other divisions were processed at Stalag IX-B. Other nationalities were incarcerated at the facility. From various areas, the amount of men constantly increased, until the non-commissioned officers and others were removed.

More trains arrived in Bad Orb. The ones, who continued, were disappointed. The journey for many men wasn't completed. A few continued to die, as the days passed, until all arrived at their appropriate destination.

If trains moved deeper inside Germany, the daylight hours were used. More defenses were available for protection. The speed was also increased to save time. The main concentration of prisoners wasn't hindering their progress.

Many of the prisoner's determination to withstand the horror increased but some reached their limits of endurance. The burdens needed to be overcome. No choice existed for anyone, except life or death.

Chapter Seven: The Death March

The train arrived at the prison camp. The men were relieved to finally reach their destination. All were weak from the journey. Each boxcar was unlocked and then the prisoners began to exit. The length of the confinement affected their mobility. Many stumbled, as they stepped down from the boxcar.

The ones, who were wounded or ill, were taken to the infirmary and the dead were buried.

All the men had beards and were dirty from their confinement.

They were within the darkness for a long period of time. Sensitivity to light caused problems. The sun glared and the brightness overwhelmed their vision. Most covered their eyes while others squinted. Soreness was common. All had to adjust to the brightness.

All the men were processed.

Many barracks were used to house the prisoners. The amount of men within these structures varied. The number of men assigned to the units exceeded recommended limits.

Overcrowding was common.

All the 12 wooden structures were similar in construction.

Other buildings were within the enclosed compound, such as the infirmary, solitary, and storage buildings. The residence of the guards and commandant were outside the internal fencing. Eight guard towers were spaced along the barbed wired perimeter.

Segregation of certain soldiers did exist within nationalities, races, and religions.

The men in the barracks were in two sections on either of a washroom. The bunks had no mattresses. The men slept on wooden slats, which caused bedsores. Many slept on the floor. The buildings were built off the ground to prevent tunneling. There was only cold water and one latrine. One stove was in each section with a limited amount of firewood, per day.

A few windows were broken and the ceilings leaked.

An infirmary was available for the captives who needed attention. The medical personnel of the Allies manned this area. The proper medicines were scarce. Many died time from malnutrition.

Other diseases were prevalent. Lice, diarrhea, bedbugs, and influenza were common within the cramped living quarters. Many of the men developed various symptoms. Nothing could be done for certain illnesses. The men either improved or died from their conditions.

If the men were lucky, one blanket was received for warmth.

The meals weren't satisfactory.

The ones, who were incarcerated for long periods, showed the effects of the diet. Bread, potatoes, coffee, and soup were the main types of food. The bread was usually hard and the soup watery. Without proper nourishment, the men became weaker.

The cooks were P.O.W.'s, who were supervised by the Germans.

Many only received one humanitarian package, per 3 soldiers. Others received nothing. Very useful items were contained within the box. These necessities were the difference between life and death for many soldiers.

Before reinforcements arrived, the defenders of Bastogne were constantly shelled.

On the 26th of December, American tanks arrived and a fierce battle erupted with the Germans for three weeks until the city was safe. The men barely held their ground and survived even with the parachute drop on the 23rd.

When the tanks were seen, the survivors cheered.

Sergeant Messmer was weak from the journey. His spirit was strong but like the other men, morale decreased, as their confinement continued. There was no chance to escape. All had to accept their fate and pray for liberation.

The barracks were segregated. Nationality and race were important issues to the Germans. The Jews and Black soldiers had their own sections, as other groups. These areas were fenced and confined within certain areas of the prison.

As Sergeant Messmer and a few others entered the barracks, all glanced around the room. It was enormous with high ceilings. Wooden beams, which were spaced about 12 feet apart, were supporting the roof. The triple-decker bunks were vertically aligned in rows. The floor consisted of wooden planks. The air was chilled.

The odor reminded him of the boxcar.

"My name is Staff Sergeant Bob Jones. We have bunks for all of you," he said, as he pointed toward a few available spaces.

"Disgusting,"" said Sergeant Messmer. "Should be condemned."

"It was," said one of the other prisoners, as he was lying in his bunk. "Someone had to use it." He turned his body away from the new arrivals.

"My home is where I reside," said the Sergeant. Before he began to walk toward his bunk, he stated, "Camp Carson in Salina, Kansas was my favorite camp. I loved it. On the weekend, I traveled home on leave."

"I was assigned to that camp for a while," the Staff Sergeant stated.

"Do you remember the long "horizontal wooden plank" ramp toward the door of the barracks?"

"Yes, you're right," he replied. "Nice place."

As the Sergeant again looked in different directions, he said, "All our camps looked like heaven to this hell. After lowering his head, he continued by sadly saying, "My home with my parents, brothers, and sisters is best."

The Staff Sergeant showed the men their assigned areas.

"We just barely survive," Staff Sergeant Jones stated. "This is everyone's home, for now. All of you will adapt. All of us must adapt or die."

"How long have you been here?' asked one of the new arrivals.

"About a month. I was captured on a recon patrol. Conditions here are miserable at best. A few of our medics are staffing the infirmary. Proper medications are scarce. Maybe, with the influx of prisoners more medical personnel will be available to treat the sick and injured. We make do. There's only cold water in the washroom to clean up and shave. Maybe, I can find some bread and meat. It's tough horse meat, but edible."

"I appreciate your kindness," said Sergeant Messmer, as he slowly lowered himself on the bunk. "Just let me rest, for now."

"Anything is better than the boxcar," one of the others stated. "My feet feel like dead weight. They've never been this numb. Nothing could be worse." He removed his boots. "Just too much standing. We all need a rest."

One of the other arrivals said, "Amen to that."

After lying in their bunks for a while, the men finally washed and shaved their beards.

No new clothes were issued. Some Germans confiscated coats, clothing, and personal belongings on route to Geroelstein. Many men walked without shoes and improvised with rags on their feet. All had to make do with what they had. The Germans needed the items for their men.

The Americans suffered for their adversaries disrespect.

The air was cold within the barracks. The allotment of firewood for each stove was low. One stove was only adequate to warm the room for a limited number of hours, per day. The wood was properly used to prolong the warmth and never wasted. After the wood was consumed, the iron stoves retained heat for a short time. All of the men were chilled even with the heat.

Even a little warmth was a blessing and better than nothing.

Not too many activities existed. Lectures and bible studies were popular activities. Church services were conducted in the barracks. Card games were played. The men talked about their families and themselves. For the most part, the men stayed in bed.

All were bored with their captivity.

Many became ill from the food and other diseases. These men needed bed rest. The close living quarters amplified their conditions and caused other men to be susceptible to illnesses. With malnutrition, their immune systems weren't functioning properly.

Many vermin infested the barracks. The men helped each other pick the lice out their hair. Each man helped groom the other, when necessary. All depended on each other to survive.

The weather was still cold and snow covered the landscape in January of 1945. Outside activities were virtually nonexistent. The men spent almost all of their time within the barracks. Weakness overwhelmed all the men.

One time, after consuming food, Sergeant Messmer became ill. He was taken to the infirmary. The problem was food poisoning from the greens in the soup. They were contaminated. Upset stomachs and diarrhea were common symptoms of this condition.

"You'll be fine," said the Doctor. "The symptoms will pass."

As the Sergeant was lying on a bed, like the others in the ward, he stated, "Hope so. I never felt, so bad. Worse upset stomach; I ever had."

"Spoiled greens," said the Doctor. He glanced at the chart, while he stood beside the bed. "The quality of the food is not fit for a dog. Scuttlebutt has it; the Allies embargo is having an effect. We're not immune to the results. The prisoners are just too much of a burden on the Germans."

The Doctor walked away from him.

The Sergeant turned his head toward a man, who was in the bunk next to him. After observing him for a few moments, he stated, "How are you doing, soldier?"

No response was received, so the Sergeant continued by saying, "What's your problem?"

The other man slowly turned his head, and then replied, "Just weak, like the others. I've been imprisoned too long. Being killed on the battlefield was better than suffering in this hellhole. I want to die. Oh, God let me die."

After staring toward the man, no words could be spoken by the Sergeant. He thought that he might become like him with no hope. A quicker death may have been better than to suffer.

His thoughts were still confused.

Life was so precocious and the Germans wanted dominance to destroy anyone who opposed them. The ones, who weren't, like them, were worthless. No tolerance existed within their regime. All were disposable for their acquisition of wealth and power. Societies were crushed and forced to submit. Foolishness accelerated beyond reason.

When the Sergeant awoke, the man in the next bed was gone. The doctor told him later, the man passed away a few hours, earlier. Nothing could be done. His condition weakened his spirit and organs. A peaceful death was the result.

The man was buried in the graveyard.

Men died within the prison camps. With the lack of the proper medicines and nutrition, many more could have died. The results may have been much worse. Most never lost hope. All took care of each other with the resources available.

As more men from different nationalities were captured, the conditions became worse. The capacity of the prison camp in January 1945 was being exceeded. More and more men were arriving, which caused serious problems.

The Germans didn't anticipate the mass surrenders. Not enough facilities were prepared. The situation needed evaluation. Only basic necessities were needed to incarcerate the captives. Priorities were shifted toward the German forces. Time was needed to shuffle the prisoners and balance the overcrowding.

The battle still raged in January. The influx of men and equipment substantially increased, since December. Supplies were being air dropped and shipped to various locations.

The momentum of the Germans was decreasing.

On January 15th, one convoy was on a road, when an explosion was heard. One of the trucks was damaged from an explosion. Land mines blocked the convoy by a bridge. Two men decided to act from the 424th. One man was a Second Lieutenant and another an enlisted man.

Both carefully used bayonets to find the devices.

When artillery fire impacted their position, the convoy began to pull back to a safer location. Both men slowly and carefully continued to stick their bayonets into the soil to clear the road of the hazards.

As the shelling became too intense, the Second Lieutenant yelled, "Jump into the water under the bridge!"

When the shelling subsided, the men continued to dig out the mines. Explosions still occurred. When necessary, they continued to run for safety. Under the pressure of the artillery, they were relentless. As each device was discovered, it was removed from the road.

"Stay low!" yelled the Second Lieutenant, as shells exploded in the distance. "Focus on the land mines!"

Both men were under extreme stress. Their faces showed tension. As each bomb exploded, anxiety was becoming more prevalent. The task was their main concern, even if death was the outcome.

The process was slow and tedious.

Even without the bombardment, the job was hazardous. They concentrated on each discovery. With the explosions around their position, the objective was difficult. If mishandled, the mines could detonate at any time. Either one could be easily killed from the shelling.

Under the risk of being killed, the two men removed 27 mines from the road, which enabled the vehicles to proceed to the front.

Hitler overextended himself, which caused the Germans to eventually retreat to the Siegfried Line. The battle lasted until the end of January 1945, which killed and wounded over 100,000 thousand on both sides.

Rank was another segregation method. Certain men needed to be transferred to other prison camps to relieve the pressure. The higher-ranking officers were considered more intelligent. They were given certain privileges.

On January 25, 1945, the count at IX-B reached 4,070 prisoners. This was the highest amount of men, who were confined, before some were moved. The capacity was too much to handle and a solution was needed. Men were transferred between camps, which was based on rank and manual labor needs.

Certain prisoners were told that they would be transferred.

The noncommissioned officers would go to Stalag IX-A. The high-ranking officials were marched 100 kilometers to Stalag LXIV in Poland. The Corporals, and Privates, etc., who were physically fit, stayed for forced labor needs or were taken to other areas for work detachments. The ones, who couldn't be moved, stayed, until they could be sent to the appropriate areas.

Different methods were used to transfer the men.

Many were taken on boxcars to other camps. Others were less fortunate. Not enough boxcars were available, which may have been due to Allied bombings or priority issues by the Germans. Some were required to walk in the snow and cold weather. A great burden existed for the men. No matter the method of transport, all were miserable, but the chances for death substantially increased with the second method.

Many soldiers didn't remember what specific camps were involved in their incarceration. Some may have been moved to other areas.

Sergeant Messmer thought; the first camp was 35 miles west of Berlin. Someone could have told him that information or he may have been correct. Current maps show no prison camp in that area. Most of the men from the 106th were taken to Stalag IX-B.

Depending on certain factors, some men may have been taken to other prison camps, before being transferred, a month later, to the appropriate facilities.

The noncommissioned officers, who walked, which included Sergeant Messmer, began their trek in one of the worst German winters. Snow was everywhere and the weather was freezing. As they began their journey, misery awaited them.

More than one group walked. Others experienced the same hardship. None knew what awaited them. Each day was a test of survival. The journey seemed to be endless, because, as the lines shifted, they traveled into a nightmare.

The men began their journey on the roads within miserable weather conditions. Many inches of snow covered their path and the air was freezing. All the groups marched about 20 to 25 miles a day. All the men's feet were wet. As they continued, their legs became weaker. Faces and hands became numb. All were weak from the elements and previous experiences.

No blankets were issued.

The clothes on their backs were their only protection from the elements. Some had jackets, but others had only the basics, such as shirts and pants. While some had boots, others didn't. The less fortunate used rags for their feet. None had the proper attire for the brutal conditions.

All the men thought, only about a week was needed to arrive at Stalag IX-A. To everyone's surprise, the march continued. The path of the prisoners changed because the Allies were on the offensive. The trail seemed to never end.

The destination became unknown to everyone.

Sergeant Messmer and the others marched 2 abreast. About 100 men began the journey with this group and all wanted the ordeal to end. The weather and diet caused their strength to subside. The hardship was overbearing and the men helped each other.

American and British soldiers marched.

The food was worse than the prison camp. The Germans gave them 2 pieces of bread and 2 pieces of lunchmeat for a two days supply. The bread was hard. The lunchmeat wasn't satisfying.

All the men were starving.

One day, as they walked, the men noticed a beet field in the distance. Even with the risk of being killed, all of them ran toward it. Many of the men began to harvest the beats and eat them. No one thought of being killed.

Their hunger needed to be satisfied.

The Germans guards just stood and watched. They knew the men weren't trying to escape. As they observed them, many laughed. Maybe, they thought; the prisoners were humiliating themselves. Others knew the outcome of their desires. None of the guards interfered. The Germans knew the outcome, since the beets were raw and spoiled.

The ones, who participated of the feast, developed dysentery for a week. With the lack of proper nourishment and no medicine, the illness was prolonged and more severe. The men became even weaker. There was no relief. The men continued their odyssey and relieved themselves during rest stops, or as they marched, which caused more problems without proper sanitation.

"How long will this march continue?" asked Sergeant Messmer. "Is there no end?"

Another Sergeant replied, "They want us all to die. I can't take it anymore. I want to be free!"

The man broke formation and began to run into the field. There was no chance of escape. His fear caused him to exhibit irrational behavior. No one blamed him or the others who ran. Too many needed to escape the misery of hell.

One of the German guards aimed his rifle toward the man and fired. He staggered a few more feet and dropped in the snow. As the men watched, nothing could be done. No movement was seen. The soldier seemed to be dead.

The men marched into the distance as the body was left in the snow.

"We should be resting for the night," said Staff Sergeant Bob Jones. "My feet have had it."

The German soldiers eventually directed the men toward a barn in the distance.

All found a place of rest, before they continued the next day. The barn had no heat and the men no coverings, except for hay and the body warmth of the other soldiers. All appreciated the time to sleep but sometimes a few never awoke.

The same routine was occurring every day.

Men were dying by dropping in the road, shot by the Germans, and dying at night. If a person ran, they were killed. The Germans usually kicked the ones, who fell, so they would continue. Many times, the person was left for dead or shot. Sleep brought death to a few in the barns and warehouses. Every morning one or more men were dead from exposure and malnutrition.

The Germans allowed the prisoners to bury the ones, who died during the night.

All of the men wanted to finish the journey. Their determination was strong. The conditions showed no respect for anyone. Eventually, all could die. The weak and the ones, who lost hope, were the first. The cause of death was from the elements and the treatment by the Germans.

No one wanted to be killed, if they tried anything foolish or fell in the road.

Endurance levels were exceeded by a few, who abolished reason, and were killed for their efforts. The fear of death prevented the others from losing hope. Death claimed many of the others without warning as their strength departed. There was no comfort in sleep, until death brought the final rest for the ones, who never awoke.

The men huddled together at night and held each other. At least, with the sun, some warmth existed. The day had many facets of wind and wetness. At night, the air was different. The cold was stagnating and every advantage was needed to sustain life. The men helped each other, while walking and sleeping.

Survival depended on a team effort.

One by one the men began to fall as they continued toward an unknown destination. Some, after being kicked and beaten, were shot, and others left to die. The mood of the guard and maybe their orders determined the fate of the fallen. A few guards may have shown mercy. The randomness of the brutal acts gave the prisoners a time to ponder their fate. None of the men wanted to fall, but as their strength departed, only one final choice remained.

"We've been chosen to die," said one of the Master Sergeants, as he hung on another soldier.

Sergeant Messmer, who was holding Staff Sergeant Jones, stated, "The dirty Krauts are miserable, like us, in this weather. They could shoot all of us, if they wanted us dead."

"We'd be better off," said the Staff Sergeant. "At least, they have the proper clothes and food."

A group of men could be seen in the distance. They were approaching from the opposite direction. All the men wore black stripes and seemed just as tired as the Americans. All were malnourished. The count was about 50 men.

None of the Americans understood what they were observing.

With wonderment, Sergeant Messmer asked, "Who are they?"

"I don't know," replied Staff Sergeant Jones.

"Strange uniforms," said another soldier.

As the columns of men passed each other, no emotion was seen. A few of the men, who walked past the Americans, turned toward them with pitiful expressions. Confusion was within the soldier's thoughts. They wondered, who these men were, and where they were traveling. Some may have understood, but didn't express their feelings. The columns of men passed each other without further comment.

While the Americans walked, they continued to converse with each other.

"I wonder what happened to my men," said Sergeant Messmer. "Good bunch."

"Manual labor," Staff Sergeant Jones stated. "The Krauts need every available man. Our boys do the dirty jobs, which contributes to their war effort."

"If I ever have children," Sergeant Messmer said, " I don't want them to know anything about what happened. I pray to God; I could forget."

While they continued to hold each other, the Staff Sergeant stated, "No one should ever forget the sacrifice of the ones, who died."

Sergeant Messmer said, "One Kraut was split into. As parts of his body fell, his heart was still beating. We had to kill them. I have no compassion for any of them. For our men, we did what we had to do." He briefly trembled, before saying, "The killing is quick but the memories linger."

"The Krauts were the aggressors," said the Staff Sergeant. I have no regrets, either. You're right. It will be difficult to live with. The images will always be burnt within me. I don't know, if I can live with those thoughts. We chopped them up, like chord wood. Just sickening."

Both men staggered with the others.

"We're trapped, until the journey ends," said Sergeant Messmer. "The ones, who ran, had no chance. Hope only sustains everyone. Does this path lead to death or salvation?"

"About half are no longer with us," replied the Staff Sergeant. "For 30 days we marched. Many good men perished. Their wives and families will never know what happened, if none survive. All of us may be forgotten."

"As time passes, none of us will be remembered," said another Sergeant." No one will remember our names."

Sergeant Messmer painfully said, "I'm too weak. My legs and feet are totally numb." He stumbled, as the Staff Sergeant tried to support him. "Just no more strength."

The Staff Sergeant said, "Hold on." He tried to readjust his grip, as the Sergeant began to fall toward the ground. "Stand up." He tried to pull him up. After the Sergeants knees touched the road, he fell forward.

No movement was visible and he appeared to be dead.

Guards approached and signaled the Staff Sergeant to continue and leave the man. As the prisoners marched past the area, one of the guards nudged the Sergeant with his rifle. Many of the man turned, while the Germans stood by the body. All were ready to hear him being beaten or a gunshot, but no sounds were heard.

German soldiers looked toward the body. There was no compassion. If life still existed, the elements would kill him. The rifle was pointed away from the man. The German guards stood by the body.

As others walked past him, the Sergeant lay in the road, as dead.

His journey was completed. Weakness overwhelmed him. He couldn't move, but even if he could, there was nowhere to go. The misery, which he felt, was no longer relevant, as he waited for a peaceful death.

He felt nothing except his life drifting into oblivion.

After a brief period, he heard voices. Two British soldiers from the rear of his group broke formation and tried to help. He heard the British accents. A few turned over his body. After gradually opening his eyes, he saw a group of men around him.

Even if the Germans wanted to leave him in the road to die, a few of the British prisoners insisted on helping him. Since they accepted the responsibility, the Germans relented.

"Poor chap," said one of the men. "He looks like bloody hell."

"Lucky to be alive," said another British soldier. "All the others were dead."

The German guards allowed them to place the Sergeant in a wagon. They continued to escort the men to the prison camp. It was only a few miles in the distance. The two British prisoners pulled the wagon toward the end of the journey. Even with their weakened condition, the extra weight was not a hardship.

The course was finished for the Sergeant. The rest was a relief. After 30 days, he lost his strength at the proper time. He would not proudly walk into the prison camp. Very little pride existed because all were worn and spirits depressed. The success of the journey was from the power of others, who cared. The help was appreciated. From the compassion of others, he survived.

Survival was the only prideful emotion.

"Don't worry, Sergeant," said another British soldier, as he walked next to the wheel. "You'll be fine. After noticing a strange odor, he said, "Blimey, you smell like rotten garbage. I suppose; we all need a shower and shave. We'll all be cleaned up in know time. Don't worry. Just rest. Boy, are you a lucky bugger. The guard could have shot you. If the Germans didn't allow us to help, you'd be a goner."

The Sergeant turned his head and stared toward the British soldier. Death was averted again. He couldn't understand. Too many have died. He wasn't stronger than any other man.

The grenade didn't explode and the machine gun jammed. The man above him in the boxcar was killed and now he was saved from certain death. The only explanations were luck or divine intervention. The others were more worthily to be spared. He perceived nothing special about himself.

The primary emotion; he felt, was relief, even if he was distressed.

Many did die but he was spared. Nothing else was important for the moment. His misery for this ordeal ended. The next step awaited him. Even if the prison camp was as miserable as the first, he began to appreciate what he had. Never look back, he thought. Always live for the moment and be blessed for what is given, whether it was good or bad.

While the war raged, no one was safe.

Death could come at any moment. All would die, eventually from the war, natural causes, diseases, disasters, murder, or old age. He didn't now how long he would live. If there was something at the end of the journey, he wanted it.

If the true God was revealed to him, there was more to gain.

All he knew was pomp and ceremony. Hollowness existed within him. He needed the love of God to fill his heart. A personal relationship was necessary.

The attitude, symbols, and hierarchy of the church repulsed him, but he knew nothing else. He was Catholic, even if he didn't attend church, as much as he should. Something else must

exist.   The church wouldn't preach heresy.
There was nothing wrong with anyone
worshipping God.   All had different methods for
the same result.   If there was a single truth, he
wanted it, but where would he find it.

He was brought to the camp infirmary.

The medical personnel treated him.
Frostbite and hypothermia were his main
problems with swollen feet.   After his boots were
cut off, he was treated, given food, and rested for
many days.   The beard was removed and a
shower was taken, as he began to feel better.
New clothes were issued.   His spirits were
uplifted and the past seemed a distant memory.

He was assigned to a barracks, which was
an improvement from the other prison camp.
The "A" camp was for the noncommissioned
officers.   It was still bad with lousy food but the
weather improved.   Showers were available
outside the barracks.   The amount of men
incarcerated was less than the first facility.

Overcrowding was not an issue.

The coming spring season was a good
time of year, which brought newness.   More
books were available to read and the
overcrowding was minimized.   Lectures and
bible studies were available by the Chaplin.

No one could imagine the horrendous
conditions in which these men lived.   Although
the noncommissioned officers were treated
better in many respects than the ones, below
their rank, conditions were still miserable.

All the men lost weight from the improper
diet.

Outdoor activities were mostly not utilized,
because of the men's weakened condition.

Many, who walked to the prison camp, had bad feet. Their strength was limited from malnourishment. Depression was prevalent with many of the captives.

Chapter Eight: Liberation

The conditions weren't much better than the first camp but the changing season brought hope. The air was becoming warmer and the snow was melting. As spring approached, the conditions in the barracks were more tolerable. Although most stayed in their bunks, many did walk outside during warmer days. Many men read books. Others played cards and attended bible study, religious services, and other lectures in their assigned areas.

Showers were available on the outside of barracks.

All the men continued to help each other. Those, who had more strength, took care of those, who needed help. The weight of the men decreased during their captivity from the improper diet. Very few were physically active. The ones with frostbite had trouble walking. The spirits of many men were depressed. Illnesses and lice still plagued all the captives. As the men lay in bed, bed soars increased. Even in weakened conditions, all cared for one another.

One time, Sergeant Messmer, like the other men, helped the ones in need.

There was a man, who needed water. Even with his bad feet and feeble condition, he walked toward the man. After comforting him, he grabbed a bucket and slowly walked outside. As the guards watched, he gradually proceeded toward a well in the common area. His feet dragged and he stumbled a few times. The bucket was filled and he returned to the barracks.

The man was grateful and was refreshed.

The men all wondered when the war would end. The only information was from the Germans and the newer prisoners. All the men thought that they would die, before help arrived. They were the lucky ones, who continued to survive.

Life was being drained from their existence.

As Sergeant Messmer lay on his bunk, he continued to contemplate his life.

When the war was over, he wanted to find a good woman. None of the women; he knew, wanted a serious relationship. Many said that he was very attractive, but he never encouraged them. Too many women wanted him for the wrong reason.

The boundaries of propriety were the motivating factor. All the relationships were just empty shells. Although he enjoyed the attention, none of the women had the proper qualities for marriage.

All the women were just momentary distractions. The hollowness of his life needed to be replaced with something better. Strength and courage were the main attributes of his search. Other vital factors were stability and an inner peace. He wanted a different type of woman. The past needed be buried for a new type of life with joy and goodness.

The beauty of a woman was only temporary. Everyone declined both physically and mentally. The strength came from within and was based off of a true love. The outer shell was just a façade to hide the truth. If nothing of value existed from the inner core, then the mask was worthless. Loveliness came from a deeper understanding.

The Sergeant was cocky with his decisions. The young took risks. Until death approached, too many thought that they were invincible. The courage; he exhibited was beyond the call of duty. His squad depended on him for leadership. His behavior was risky. Nothing else could be done. If he and the Staff Sergeant didn't act, all the squad was at risk of death.

Staff Sergeant Waller was a good friend.

Both had many good times in the States and England. Neither wanted to fight in this horror. Duty was the only option to kill the Germans for survival. The experience was horrifying.

In an instant, his friend was dead from a risky maneuver. No specific person was to blame. Both men knew the risks and evaluated the options. The savagery of war was the cause. Men on both sides wanted to live and all were performing their duty.

When leaders make decisions, the innocent and guilty suffer.

He wondered, if the memories would ever be forgotten. The current horror within his mind was unable to contemplate what the future would reveal from the past. Memories faded over time and were replaced by newer experiences. Other priorities needed to suppress the past; otherwise the past would haunt him, until he died.

The war needed to end and if the Germans, who were killed by the Sergeants hand, saved American lives, he was satisfied. When the war ended, the experiences should begin to subside, over time. If the memories continued, the war would never end within him. The void needed to be filled. The conflict was disturbing between what needed to be done and the results of his actions.

The Chaplains and others conducted lectures about the bible and other subjects within the barracks. With the men's weakened condition, nothing else could be done, except for talking, listening, reading books, and playing cards. Most of the time was spent inside the buildings, except for roll call, obtaining water, and showers. When the weather became warmer, many prisoners walked into the common area with more frequency to enjoy the fresh air.

Only a few had some physical activity in the courtyard.

All were allowed outside the barracks between certain hours.

A few of the guards were nicer than others. Some were more hostile but all were required to follow orders. Anyone could be disciplined, if the rules weren't followed. Some guards thought; the conditions were deplorable at the prison camp. Most didn't care for their duties and treated the prisoners with malice and disrespect.

"When will we be freed?" asked a man in a bunk, as he threw a playing card toward his boot. The Ace of Spades fell upright on the wooden floor. "My wife and kids give me hope."

In an opposite bunk, Sergeant Messmer said, "Bill, only the Lord knows," He held a cigarette between his fingers. "Just leave everything in his hands and pray. He is watching over us." He placed it in his mouth, inhaled a few times, and then blew smoke in the air.

Staff Sergeant Banister stated, "I should have died with my men in combat, if there was no hope for survival. Better to die with honor, than to die, needlessly." He threw another card, which also missed its mark. "If I am allowed to caress and kiss her again, I would do anything for the experience."

"What's your wife's name?" asked another soldier, who lay in his bunk above him.

"Betty Washington Banister. My children names are Carl and Michele."

"Nice names," he replied.

"Very faithful wife," the Staff Sergeant stated. "I worked long hours to support them. Sometimes, I felt that I was neglecting my family to profit the company and my own pockets." He briefly paused, before saying, "My occupation is car sales. Hard business. Standards are difficult to obtain without fudging the truth and sometimes blatantly lying. The company doesn't endorse the selling techniques. The sale practices are just ignored for the bottom line, unless a serious complaint is received. I wonder, if my family was informed? With the propaganda of the Third Reich, no one probably knows how we're being treated."

"What can we do?" Sergeant Messmer asked. "Worrying will solve nothing. This is our home. We'll either return to our families or eventually die in this sickening pit. While we're alive, there's hope. All of us are trapped. There is no chance of escape."

None of the prisoners from the camp attempted to leave the compound. They were too weak and their specific location was unknown. None of them had a chance to return to the lines. All would have been recaptured or killed. Common sense prevailed. Even if the conditions were miserable, all decided to wait for freedom from the advancing troops.

With other escape attempts within the homeland, Germany tightened the rules. Posters were displayed throughout the camp about the new policy. It stated: "To All Prisoners of War: Germany has always kept to the Hague Convention and only punished recaptured prisoners of war with minor disciplinary punishment. Germany will still maintain these principles of international law. But England has besides fighting at the front in an honest manner instituted an illegal warfare in non-combat zones in the form of gangster commando's terror bandits and sabotage troops even up to the frontiers of Germany...in plain English stay in the camp, where you will be safe! Breaking out of it is now a damned dangerous art...All police and military guards have been given the most strict orders to shoot on sight all suspected persons."

"Where would we go?" asked the Staff Sergeant.

"No where," the First Sergeant replied. His name was Jerry Grayson. He momentarily leaned over his bunk, and then continued, "There's noting we can do. Without help, we would die or be killed."

After placing his hand on the bedpost, the Staff Sergeant said, "I was talking to someone, who said; their First Lieutenant in another division charged toward the enemy with all his platoon. Very bold frontal-assault maneuver."

The First Sergeant became agitated.

"Foolish," Sergeant Messmer stated with the cigarette in his mouth. "I wanted to stay and fight." He removed it, before saying, "All of us would have been killed. We killed, so many of those Krauts, I thought they were bluffing. Their numbers and arsenals were too massive. I was wrong but I wanted to kill all of them. I thought that we could handle the attack like many others."

"Their First Lieutenant was killed and many of his men," said the Staff Sergeant. "Before he died, he was signaling toward his men to continue. The enemy was defeated. Maybe, he prevented more deaths."

The First Sergeant stated, "No one can judge his actions. He was in command and did what he thought was appropriate, like anyone else. Maybe, he was foolish. If he had a family, will a medal for courage or foolishness sustain them?"

"You're right," the Staff Sergeant stated. "The military will probably give him a medal. A Private in the 589th; I was told, ran toward an M-8 armored car, after the turret gunner was wounded. He told the driver to obtain a better position of the enemy in a nearby house. As the vehicle moved, he stood and fired upon the enemy stronghold. His gun jammed a couple of times, but he fixed the problem and continued to fire. About 20 of the Krauts were killed and their position was neutralized. To save lives, something needed to be done, even if death resulted."

Before flicking the remaining portion of the cigarette in a water bucket, Sergeant Messmer stated, "I don't want any medals. Although we had to kill for survival, glorifying violence with awards is not what I want. I may have killed a dozen or maybe 30 or 40. I don't know. Blood and body parts were everywhere. They came and we killed. We had no choice. There was no time to think.

If lives were in danger, they needed to be killed. I'd kill all of them again to prevent more violence. I'd rather find the proper road to heaven, if hell were worse than what I saw. The trees, men, and vehicles were burning. As fire consumed their lives, many Krauts screamed for help. Some of my boys were shocked at the carnage. Nothing could be done, except wait, until their bodies fell to the ground and continued to burn. Their skin just melted away. Smoldering and burnt flesh was all that remained."

"There was a Captain in the 28th infantry, who refused to evacuate, because of his frozen and crippled feet," said the Staff Sergeant. "He constantly sought better positions for his men to attack the enemy. He went from squad to squad to encourage the men until the enemies advance ceased."

"John, did you do anything?" asked First Sergeant Grayson.

"You mean, Bill, besides wanting to stay on the hill and fight?"

"Yes," he replied.

"None of your business," said Sergeant Messmer. "I did what I had to do, like anyone else. No glory exists in war and death. Someday, my acts will fade into oblivion. None of us were heroes. If I have children, someday, none will know the truth. My younger brother, Jake, will probably pester me, like my other brothers and sisters. Maybe, telling someone will help with the agony. I just want to forget. I pray to God; the horror within me will be extinguished. I was almost killed three times." He began to shake, before saying, "The grenade could have blew my head off." After a brief silence, his anguish diminished, before he continued his words, "One war is enough for me, but I'd fight again for my family to protect them. None of my children will experience this nightmare. I'd go in their place."

The First Sergeant smiled, and then said, "The military wouldn't let you."

"Too bad," he replied, "Even with what happened, I'd go to protect them."

"After all the death and destruction," stated Staff Sergeant Banister, "war will be less tolerated, but power hungry madmen will always exist." Another card was thrown. "Too many people want control of others and their wealth. If submission doesn't occur, conflicts erupt. No one will ever be at peace."

"Suppose not," Sergeant Messmer said. "A true inner peace is difficult to find. Yes, but maybe the void can be filled." He paused, slightly smiled, and then asked, "Anymore acts of bravery?"

A few other soldiers walked past their bunks.

"I heard that a Private in the 423rd rushed a machine gun nest," the Staff Sergeant replied, "A grenade knocked them unconscious. He was killed, when the Germans opened fire from another hidden position."

"When people are old, they can reminisce," Sergeant Messmer stated. "Maybe, war stories are what army buddies have in common in their old age. Everyone will say how brave; they were." He moved into a different position on his bunk and groaned.

"Back bothering you?" asked the Staff Sergeant, as he flipped another card toward his boot.

"With my bed soars, I can't want to sleep on a fluffy mattress," the Sergeant replied. "I used to fantasize about other things. Strange. Priorities change."

"Amen to that," said the First Sergeant. "A cold foamy beer with a medium rare juicy steak and a buttery potato are my current desires."

Sergeant Messmer stated, "My mom used to make a great potato salad."

"Really," said the Staff Sergeant. "My Mom made the best tomato sauce for her homemade ravioli. Delicious." He reached for the cards on the floor, picked up each one, and then asked, "John, what did you do, before the war?" He began to momentarily shuffle the cards, before placing the stack on the bunk.

"Window washer at a Club in St Louis," he replied. "Under the GI Bill, they're supposed to hire me back. I really loved it there. I don't know what the future holds, really. Being a window washer all my life is not what I want. With a grade school education, options are limited. Not too much that I could do. God will make a way."

"Someday, high school will be required for everyone," stated First Sergeant Grayson. "College is just a fantasy. The GI Bill does provide training and educational opportunities."

The Sergeant rubbed his hands, before saying, "I may try something different after the war. All will be known in time."

A man approached them and said, "There's a bible study, this afternoon, in the western corner of the barracks. Everyone's invited."

"Everyone enjoys your teachings, Chaplin," said the Staff Sergeant. "Most informative. Your congregation is always in the chapel. No one else to go."

Even in their weakened condition, many of the men briefly laughed and others smiled.

"I still want to preach to the Negro soldiers but the Germans refused my request again," said the Chaplin. "There's nothing; I can do. I am afraid that they will be taken away to labor camps.

Many of you may remember; the Jewish soldiers were sent elsewhere from Stalag IX-B to God knows where. I heard some unbelievable and horrible stories. If true, we are battling the devil. The inhumanity disturbs me." He pushed the hair from his eyes. "The Jews were required to report for segregation at the beginning of January. I am proud of the boys, who stopped them from submitting to the order, until the Germans became stricter with the policy. All of the Jews, who refused to comply, would have been killed, if discovered."

"How do the Germans know?" asked the Staff Sergeant.

"For some reason, the Jews volunteer the information," said the Chaplin. "A person's name might disclose their identity. Some talk too much. Informants. He glanced toward a few of the men, and then said, "I don't understand their willingness to disclose such things."

"What are we fighting for?" asked Sergeant Messmer. "They are men, like us. They fought for the same cause. Give them the word of God. Find a way."

"Do they need a preacher?" asked First Sergeant Banister.

Chaplin Rice inquisitively asked, "What do you mean?"

"Don't they have any bibles? Let them choose someone."

"Yes, but it's highly inappropriate," replied the Chaplin. "Order must be maintained. They need a true shepherd. Someone chosen by God to guide them."

"Baloney!" shouted the First Sergeant. "Let them be guided by the Spirit of God."

"Just preach to them by the fence," Sergeant Messmer stated. "The weather's improved."

The Chaplin briefly lowered his head, and then stated, "Many are too weak to leave their bunks. I don't know how to help them."

"Just offer a prayer," said the Sergeant.

The Staff Sergeant interrupted by saying, "Those people are in a separate area for a reason. Many of us don't want to associate with those types. Tensions may increase, which could cause trouble for us and the Germans."

"Idiot!" shouted Sergeant Messmer. "Everyone was created by God! Didn't you learn anything? Life is too precious to waste. All oppression must stop to have a permanent peace."

"Messmer is right," said the First Sergeant. "Everyone has something to offer. No one is inferior. The Nazis want control. Everyone else is useless. All they want to do is profit from the misery of others." He angrily stared toward the Staff Sergeant for a few moments, and then asked, "Should true Christians judge the destiny of others or should we love everyone, like Christ loved us by shedding his blood? We've seen too much violence to hurt anyone else."

"This horror changed all of us," Sergeant Messmer said.

After saying, "Amen," the Chaplin away from them.

The Staff Sergeant picked up his playing cards and looked at them. All were similar but different. The purpose of each had value. The game needed all the deck. No one could win just with one card. All weren't of equal value but all were equally needed. The strengths of each were necessary. Any card hand had to equally stand together for a positive outcome.

Many different types of people did serve during the war, including women. Many women were killed during bombings. They jumped into foxholes and manned weapons, when the men weren't available. Some flew planes and performed many of the same tasks, as the men. Credit was never given for their accomplishments, except for over 565 bronze stars, which were given to them in the European and Pacific conflict. When the war ended, many women were honored but never given equal treatment for their military service.

Sometimes, after Sergeant Messmer took a shower, he stayed outside the barracks for a while during warmer days. The warmth and fresh air was a relief from the misery of the winter. His mind wandered. He thought about what happened from the initial encounter with the enemy and his loving family. Life changed for him and the others. The world wasn't the same. For now, he and the others were alive. With the war raging, anything could happen to place anyone's life in jeopardy.

The nice weather increased his faith of a better tomorrow.

He stood or sat outside by the building and watched the few who were strong enough to perform minor activities. Some just walked in the fresh air. Others played games with any available objects. Since the men were losing weight from malnutrition, the exercise wasn't prolonged. Most men stayed within their bunks and rested to preserve their strength.

Not all German soldiers were evil. Many did what they were told under the threat of death, while others enjoyed their duties. Their men followed orders, as the soldiers of other nationalities followed commands.

Hitler was their leader, who forced his dictatorship on the world. Too many obeyed orders without question and ignored reason. There was no excuse for the atrocities of the regime. All the German people were responsible.

Too many people accepted the rhetoric and the biased research. The minds of the populace were corrupted. Even in a free society too many people accepted what they are told and were caught in the fervor of the moment. As the fire increased, more were burnt by corruption.

Without the true morals from God, man made values reigned and lead the unsuspecting to destruction. Even within the Christian faith, too many have corrupted the Gospel for their pleasure. Preachers have twisted the word and gained wealth from their followers, while their followers suffered the consequences. Bible verses were taken out of context to endorse tradition. The whole truth was buried behind blinders, which lead people off the true path.

Many were butchered and killed in Germany who refused to accept the abnormal behavior of a corrupt regime. Others were just the targets of a deranged mentality. Too many suffered from the greed and power of their oppressors. Anyone, who stood in the way of the Third Reich, was worthless and disposable.

With God, everyone had a purpose and was his children. When one commandment was broken, all were violated. Points were not tabulated in heaven for each sin. All sin disgusted God and was of equal measure. The way of escape was not just accepting him by our lips and acting holy. The change came from within the heart.

God only knew his children from a bonded relationship. The fruits were shown, not by good works, but by what others were shown from within. Works have lead many to destruction even if they confessed to be Christians. If people were lead by the true Spirit of God, creations of man were diminished and madness decreased.

The Allies pushed forward into Germany.

The soldiers of the Third Reich were being encircled and pushed into smaller pockets. The Russians, British, and Americans were on the offensive. Intense resistance was encountered within the Fatherland. The march toward Berlin continued, after the Germans retreated from the offensive at the end of January of 1945.

The Germans were weary and returned to their country in humiliation. Hitler's last offensive failed to ignite into a decisive victory. Moral was low and much of their equipment destroyed or damaged. Embargos helped to diminish supplies. All the troops fought with all their strength and power. Many good men were lost on both sides. Hitler didn't anticipate the freshness of the American forces and their fighting spirit.

The resistance was too strong with America's involvement in the war. The supply of troops, equipment, and weapons with the determination of the men blocked the advance.

The Germans overextended their reach and failed to recapture previous territories from their inferior position.

As the battles raged, the fighting was fierce. Layers of antagonism were peeled into oblivion. The countless bombings of occupied Germany and the invading forces continued the march. All were on the momentum except for the German forces. As the German forces were pushed into smaller regions, defenses were collapsing.

"Beautiful day," said Sergeant Messmer, as he watched a few men play catch in the courtyard with a baseball. "Will anyone ever be free?" He momentarily turned his head toward another barbed wired section of the camp, where he saw the Negro's mingling outside their barracks.

"The newer prisoners confirm eventually victory," replied Staff Sergeant Bob Jones. "The propaganda from the Germans is hogwash. If the Allies keep marching forward, Hitler will have no place to hide. The day will come, when the bells of freedom will ring for everyone."

"Maybe, all will learn from what happened," the Sergeant said. "Some memories should always remain. Only time will reveal the truth."

"All of us have prejudice and bias," stated the Staff Sergeant. "Everyone needs time to bury the past. Hatred has many root causes. Too many just accept what they are told in youth."

The Sergeant glanced toward him, and then asked, "What's on the menu, today?"

"Same, as always. Just a piece of meat and soup with hard bread."

"Maybe, the meat won't be as tough. A person can always hope."

"John, at least, with the humanitarian packages, a few basic supplies are obtained. The food, tobacco, medicine, and hygiene items are useful."

"Even one smoke a day calms my nerves. I don't know what I'd do without 'um. It's just a nasty habit. Maybe, my attention will be focused away from cigarette's with other priorities."

"Sharing a package with three people is useless," the Staff Sergeant said, "but anything helps."

"Better than nothing."

The Staff Sergeant glanced toward the guard towers. He then stated, "Everyone has lost too much weight already."

"I weighted 175 pounds, before the surrender," said Sergeant Messmer. "Now, I am skin and bones. I don't feel good." He lifted his hand and then began to feel his hair. "Even after the men pick lice from me, more return. The barracks are totally infested. The rats are waiting to pick our bones. At least, they'll have a good meal, before our bodies rot."

"Probably all the prison camps are about the same."

"I don't know," said the Sergeant. "The officers are supposed to be treated better. The men, who are used for labor detail, are probably in worse shape." He noticed one of the men drop the ball. "Butter fingers!" he yelled. "Who taught you to catch?" After turning toward the Staff Sergeant, he continued by saying, "None would be drafted on either of the St Louis teams."

As they continued to toss the ball, a few of the men in the courtyard smiled.

"Sports fan?" asked the Staff Sergeant.

"Oh, the series was a great one for the birds, last year, with a 4 game to 2 win. Just think, the two teams from St. Louis in the same series. I always enjoyed going to Sportsman's Park with my brothers or a gal. I heard parts of the series on the radio. Both are great teams. I know; more people bet on the birds to win. They're a much better franchise. Many great players were drafted from both leagues. Even with the military 4 F's, who were playing, the season was a great one. If I have children, some day, I'll take them to the games."

"Truly was an exciting season."

"What team is your favorite?"

The Staff Sergeant leaned against the wall, and then replied, "I'm from Iowa. I listen to a few games on the radio from different cities. I really don't have a preference."

"Do you really think; all prison camps are the same?" asked the Sergeant.

"In a way," the Staff Sergeant replied. "All are probably laid out the same. Barbed wire fencing, guard towers, barracks, and other buildings. This one seems to be in better shape than the other one. This place is probably newer. All are hellholes."

"At least, we're alive. Too many have died for this godforsaken war. I always wonder, if God has a plan for the ones, who survive. Maybe, we are just the lucky ones. Men stick up their heads, and then shrapnel or one bullet kills them instantly, while others run through a hail of bullets and aren't hurt. My understanding is limited."

The Staff Sergeant smiled, before saying, "Maybe, the future holds the key for everyone."

Both men with their damaged feet slowly walked into the barracks.

The days passed and their hope for freedom never wavered, even if their health worsened. Their weight continued to decrease. Diseases were still a problem for all the camps. Most of the time, the men just stayed in bed and waited. If the Allies continued to push forward, eventually they would be found alive or dead.

A birthday was approaching for Sergeant Messmer. He was going to be 29 years old on April 6, 1945. The event was pleasurable. The days were remembered with his parents, brothers, and sisters. They always remembered with a card, gifts, and a delicious cake.

His family showed much affection for each other on these special occasions.

Just before his birthday, a present was given to him and all the other men. The lines were moving closer to the area. Other camps were already liberated. The timing of this event may have just been a coincidence or a blessing from God, which would never be forgotten. Either way, the prison camp was the next one to be freed by incoming forces.

Early in the morning, a few prisoners noticed some of the guards quickly leaving. Word spread within the barracks and the men went outside to investigate. Some placed their arms around the ones, who were in worse condition, and helped them. The guards, who remained, showed panic in their faces. They stood within the compound by the open outer gate.

The guard towers were vacant.

Two British tanks could be seen in the distance. As they approached, the prisoners began to cheer and run toward the fence. The weaker prisoners were supported. The men enthusiastically waved, as the tanks approached.

No resistance was encountered because the remaining guards thought that they were outnumbered. The Germans placed their hands in the air and surrendered, as a few soldiers jumped from the tanks with their weapons.

"We're free, John!" stated First Sergeant Grayson. "My God."

Sergeant Messmer waved toward the tanks, and then stated, "It's about time!" he yelled. "Finally! I thought; we were just waiting for death. Our prayers were answered. Oh, Jesus, thank you! Show me the way of salvation."

"Just look at those beauties!" said Staff Sergeant Banister. "Wow!"

A few men ran toward the Negro soldiers compound and helped them tear down the barbed wire, as they did with the other nationalities. Those men ran from their areas toward the inner gate. It was forced open and everyone equally jumped and hugged each other.

As the Germans were told to sit in a group by the commandant's office, very little hatred was exhibited toward the Germans by most of the men. Since freedom was more of a concern, none exhibited any substantial hostility toward their captors. All were just too overjoyed with their freedom. Revenge wasn't a major concern with their weakness and ailments.

Until the camp leaders obtained the proper instructions from the advancing troops, the Germans were confined and the others stayed within the camp. Trucks were needed to transport them to medical facilities. Food was distributed, while they waited. All the men were overjoyed, even if a few had no hope for survival and others the possibilities of amputations of their damaged feet.

Most of the men were changed for the rest of their lives.

Telegrams were sent to the parents and/or wives of the men, who were liberated. The one to Sergeant Messmer stated; "The secretary of war desires me to inform you that your son Sgt Messmer, John A. returned to military control 24 April 45. Report further states, however, that he is hospitalized in European area but not due to enemy action. New address and further information follow direct from hospital. J.A. Ulio, the Adjutant General.

When Sergeant Messmer weight was checked at the hospital, 95 pounds was the reading. After the staff evaluated him, medical problems were a concern. Treatments were initiated. His condition wasn't critical, but problems existed.

Powder was sprayed all over him to kill the lice in an English Hospital. With the proper died, medications, and therapies his strength returned. Amputation was considered for his feet, which were frost bitten and swollen. Since his feet showed improvement, over time, the medical staff decided not to do the procedure, like some of the other men. He was given bed rest for about a month, before he was returned to the states on a transport plane.

He was issued new clothes and boots.

The journey toward the States caused him to be happier than he was for months. Other men accompanied him. Each man was lying on a cot. Each had individual experiences from the war. They survived and were returning home. Nothing else was important for the moment. All the horror was behind them.

After the plane landed, Sergeant Messmer reached for his new boots. To his surprise, while he slept, they were stolen. Someone aboard the plane took them. Any of the other men could have been responsible. There was noting he could do. Too many men were aboard the plane.

"I don't like thieves," Sergeant Messmer disgustingly said in a soft tone. He glanced toward his feet, and then said, "Boy, those boots were comfortable. They're all a bunch of knot heads." He looked toward the other men, who were preparing to leave the plane, and softly stated, "If I'd find him, I'd knock him down, and pull those boots off. Some people need a lesson in manners."

After spending a month in a Missouri military hospital, Fort Leonard Wood, he stayed in the army, until September 27, 1945. He was discharged from Wakeman Convalescent Hospital at Camp Atterbury. An honorable discharge was received with a BAME Rib b on 2 Stars, Good Conduct Ribbon, and a Combat Infantry Badge, plus eventually, when he was over 70 years old, a Bronze Star, like the others, who served.

The war was over with Germany and Japan.

The German troops were still fighting, even after Hitler committed suicide on April 30, 1945. Current autopsies of the bones suggest; he may have escaped, but in any case his troops continued to fight. The last organized unit in the south was about 200,000 German troops, who surrendered on April 24. As more German troops surrendered after Hitler's apparent demise, about 2 million German soldiers were transferred to Soviet custody. Most of them spent at most 10 years in Soviet prisons.

Japan surrendered on September 2, 1945 on the USS Missouri. Their leaders decided to surrender on August 15, after the Nuclear bombs were used on Hiroshima and Nagasaki. No defense was available for these powerful weapons. Whether or not the bombs needed to be used, the result was an end to the war, which broke the will and determination of the Japanese leaders for conquest.

The death and destruction vanished from my sight. The scene was beautiful. The snow, which covered the branches of trees and the landscape, was pristine. No more threats from the Nazis and Japan existed.

The war was won many years ago.

The memories of those men, who were thrown into an unexpected situation on the Siegfried Line, should never be forgotten. For without their bravery and courage, blood may still stain the landscape from little men, who use others for power and greed.

My Dad married my Mom and immediately stopped smoking. For her, and his spiritual well being, he attended a full-gospel church. After being baptized in water, he was filled with the baptism of the Holy Spirit with the evidence of speaking in tongues.

His relationship with God became personal.

In a peaceful and loving way, he was a stern father with a happy personality and a good sense of humor. The proper guidance needed to be given to his sons. One died at 8 years old of leukemia. His drinking was reduced to a few beers a week and then eventually no alcohol was consumed, except for a small amount of wine to celebrate New Year.

Medications prevented even this ritual.

Sometimes, he hummed or sang religious songs, while he worked around the house.

When I asked him about the war in my youth and in later years, he said virtually nothing about the battle. Only unrelated pieces of information were relayed about the initial encounter. Since the aftermath was more agreeable to his senses, it wasn't suppressed.

One time, when I was a child, he quickly fell on the floor in the kitchen and didn't move. I thought that he died. I told my Mom who was standing by the kitchen sink. As I began to cry, she told him not to scare me and get up. He began to laugh and raise himself from the floor.

He then said, "That's the way I did it during the war, son. I played dead."

Discernment was absent.

The only ones, who could understand the horror, were the men, who survived. War was disgusting. No endorsement of the process was needed. The minds of those, who didn't understand, would never comprehend the agony.

When he was about 85 years old, an Internet site was found, which related to the 106th division.

After a search was conducted, some men from Company F were discovered. My Dad never wanted the memories to resurface, but he relented. The recollections of the horror were forgotten over the years. Letters were sent and information gathered about the battle. None of the survivors remembered my Dad, who didn't remember any of the men.

He talked to a few of them and told each man his story without any regrets.

Before death, at age 90, he gave, on more than one occasion, the thumbs up sign for victory.

God's love caused the change.

The world was always plagued by war from hatred and power hungry men. Within everyone's heart resided evil. Peace and joy were the only replacements. Good works were not the answer.

Anyone could do many wonderful things within their lives. These superficial activities were meaningless, unless the goodness came from a higher power. Blood could stain the landscape again, unless hearts were changed.

Too many have a false Christianity.

The true God was not shown through works, but by his peace, love, joy, which manifested itself from within everyone, who received his Spirit with the evidence. These were the fruits of the Spirit. No one else knew the truth, unless they continued to the end under the proper guidance.

Even if church services were cancelled, because of the snow on March 24, 2013, the Spirit brought me happiness and peace with the knowledge; hope still existed for everyone to be transformed by the true Jesus and not by a manmade theology.

My imagination created the scene of the war from my Dad's statements, testimonies from men in Company F, and historical data. Whether everything was correct, I do not know. No one knows the truth, except the ones, who lived the experience. With the current facts, the threads are true while other scenes are just representations of the horror; all the soldiers faced.

Most of the real names of the soldiers in Company F of the 106th, 422nd regiment:

Alford, Joseph, Sergeant
Arnold, Roy, A, Private
Barnes, Marshall, Pfc
Barrow, Martin, A., T/5
Bell, Henry H., Jr., Pfc
Benardo, Peter J, Pfc
Berkelhamer, Lawrence H., Private
Blackburn, Marion
Blackmer, William B., T/5
Blair, Robert R., Pfc
Blytho, Wilton H., Pfc
Bradley, Francis E., T/5
Brock, Lewis P.
Burt, Clarence P., Sergeant
Carico, John M., TSgt
Carpenter, Miles J., Pfc
Carr, John W.
Carrof, John
Checca, Mario
Clark, John R., Staff Sergeant
Collons, John S., Private
Crook, Herbert D.
Dodson, Robert L., Staff Sergeant
Early, John W. Jr.
Eberhard, Victor J.
Elam, William W., Corporal
Ennis, Robert W., Staff Sergeant
Ferreira, Ted
Fuegi, Walter R., Pfc
Galvin, Edubijes, Pfc
Gerry, Ernest C., T/5
Goodman, Joseph E., Corporal
Grey, Elmer, J., Staff Sergeant
Griffin, John D.
Grimes, Charles H.,
Griser, William, E., Pfc
Grossbart, Sanford, M.
Hanke, Ralph E.
Hatton, Emery Richard
Hawkins, Martin H., First Sergeant

Hayes, John F., Pfc
Healy, Charles, L.
Henderson, Charles, S., Sergeant
Hidgon, Thomas J., Jr., Staff Sergeant
Honkomp, Elmer D., 1st Lieutenant
Hooks, James A., Pfc
Hughes, Harvey L., Sergeant
Humphrey, Richard J.
Jackson, James D.
Jebens, Arthur B., T5
Jehers, Arthur
Jones, James L., Sergeant
Kaczmarski, Stanley, T., Private
Kincade, Warren W.
King, Donald J., Pfc
Kinzer, Don S., Pfc
Kipnis, Mervyn B.
Krieger, Medford L., Pfc
Lasher, Saul E., Pfc
Lawlor, Martin V.
Mann, Theodore, C., Pfc
Mayberry, Paul E., Sergeant
Mays, Joseph A.
McCain, John J., Corporal
Messmer, John A., Sergeant
Mority, Albert, 1st Lieutenant
Moritz, Adolph G.
Nigro, Louis
Noreen, Leonard R., Pfc
Olafsen, Charles C., Pfc
Olson, Kurt E. T/5
Orzechowski, John F., Staff Sergeant
Pault, Joseph D.
Pever, Maxwell, Pfc
Phillips, George W., Jr., Pfc
Pierce, Waldo B.
Powell, William R., TSgt
Purdy, Edmond G.
Pysz, Stanley C., Pfc
Reed, Muiray J., Pfc
Reynolds, James
Riddle, Ira B., T/5
Rockhill, Charles E., Pfc

192

Rosen, Arthur S., Pfc
Roughgarden, William, T5
Rowe, Donald S., Pvt
Sabo, Jimmy, T/5
Schroer, Charles, J.
Schulz, Calvin A., Pfc
Sealander, Wilford A., Staff Sergeant
Sims, William T., Private
Spradlin, James M., T/5
Stanley, Totura, Jr.
Stewart, Neil F., Captain
Stover, Alfred C., Corporal
Sullivan, Charles J., T/4
Sweeney, Robert J. Corporal
Tapley, Denny L., Staff Sergeant
Tarbuck, Walter L., Pfc
Taylor, Ernest E., Pfc
Taylor, J. W.
Tetzloff, Henry F., Pfc
Tortura, Stanley
Travis, Joseph C., Jr., Pfc
Uhl, Winston
Unger, Joseph, Jr., Corporal
Vanni, Neil A.
Voglesong, Donald L.
Walsh, Thomas E.
Warnken, Robert
Weldon, Paul S., Pfc
West, Cecil T/5
Whitney, John H., TSgt
Whitner, Donald R., Pfc
Whitnew, Donald R.
Wiese, Herman J., T/5
Zquzenski, Creslow F., Private

Thank you for your sacrifice!